T0113858

# THE PRODIGAL

## Seen Through the Eyes of The Father

### WAYNE KNIFFEN

WESTBOW
PRESS®
A DIVISION OF THOMAS NELSON
& ZONDERVAN

WestBow Press books may be ordered through booksellers or by contacting:

WestBow Press
A Division of Thomas Nelson & Zondervan
1663 Liberty Drive
Bloomington, IN 47403
www.westbowpress.com
844-714-3454

Because of the dynamic nature of the Internet, any web addresses or
links contained in this book may have changed since publication and
may no longer be valid. The views expressed in this work are solely those
of the author and do not necessarily reflect the views of the publisher,
and the publisher hereby disclaims any responsibility for them.

Any people depicted in stock imagery provided by Getty Images are
models, and such images are being used for illustrative purposes only.
Certain stock imagery © Getty Images.

Scripture taken from the New King James Version® Copyright © 1982
by Thomas Nelson. Used by permission. All rights reserved.

Scripture quotations marked (NLT) are taken from the Holy Bible, New Living
Translation, copyright ©1996, 2004, 2015 by Tyndale House Foundation.
Used by permission of Tyndale House Publishers, a Division of Tyndale
House Ministries, Carol Stream, Illinois 60188. All rights reserved.

ISBN: 978-1-6642-8199-8 (sc)
ISBN: 978-1-6642-8200-1 (hc)
ISBN: 978-1-6642-8198-1 (e)

Library of Congress Control Number: 2022919709

Print information available on the last page.

WestBow Press rev. date: 10/27/2022

What does God think about you?
How does God see you?
How does God feel about you?

For Justin Wayne Kniffen, the best son a father could ask for. You are a wonderful husband to Sarah (McDonald) Kniffen—who happens to be my favorite and prettiest daughter-in-law—and an incredible dad to three beautiful children: Mallory Jane, Brady Cole, and Marshall Brock. You are also an outstanding teacher and coach. You make my heart smile, son. I love you.

# CONTENTS

# INTRODUCTION

I love to hear a good storyteller spin a yarn. Someone who is skilled at word-crafting can hold your attention for hours. They have the ability to keep you hanging on to every word, every phrase. Even when you know what you're hearing is not the truth, because it's skillfully presented, the one telling the story has your undivided attention.

No one could hold a candle to Jesus. He was in a class all by himself when it came to telling stories. He was the Master. Jesus had the innate ability to take something that was simply profound and make it profoundly simple. He could mesmerize an audience with his teaching ability. His choice of teaching methods was parables.

Simply stated, a parable is an earthly story that has a heavenly meaning: It is a type of metaphorical analogy. The Greek word for parable is *parabole*, which means to throw or lay something alongside something else for comparison. When Jesus, the Master Teacher, wanted someone to understand a heavenly truth, he would often make up an earthly story to place beside the truth he wanted them to understand. When they understood his made-up story, it made it easier to understand the truth he wanted them to comprehend.

Luke records one of the most familiar parables ever told by Jesus: the parable of the prodigal. The heavenly truth that Jesus wants us to glean from this earthy story is to understand what our heavenly Father thinks about us, how he sees us, and how he feels about us—even when we willfully make poor choices. Since this is one of the biggest issues—if not the biggest issue—Christians struggle with, it would be very beneficial to slow-walk our way through the entire fifteenth chapter of Luke. This is the purpose of *The Prodigal: Seen through the Eyes of the Father.*

You may be thinking what the majority of Christians think from time to time: Have I made too many mistakes or too big of a blunder for God to see me as his legitimate child? Have I gone so far that I've been disowned? Has he turned his back on me? Is he disappointed with me? Does he love me less now that I've made some bad decisions? No matter how badly you may have blown it by making foolish choices, God is not mad at you. He is madly in love with you. This is incredibly good news!

Your heavenly Father will never treat you in a way that is contrary to who you are. If you've had a born-from-above experience by accepting and receiving Jesus Christ as your Lord and Savior, then you are his child, and that's the way you will always be treated—even if you act out and besmirch your character. Your heavenly Father will always treat you like his child because that's who you are. If this truth ever gets inside of you, it will be a game changer. It will not give you a license to sin, as some believe, but it will free you from the desire to sin. You won't be sinless, but I am convinced you will sin less.

## An Exchange of Genetics: Spiritual DNA

> Therefore, if anyone is in Christ, he is a new creation;
> old things have passed away; behold, all things have
> become new. (2 Corinthians 5:17 NKJV)

Let these words settle into your spirit before you continue reading. When you accepted the Lord's invitation to life, you were born again (John 3:16 NKJV). To be born again literally means to be born from above. In other words, you gained a second birth date. As a believer, you have been born twice. Your first birth date is natural (physical), and your second birth date is spiritual. You had the DNA that comes from human genetics when you were born the first time. You had absolutely no say-so about that. There is nothing you can do that will ever cause you to lose your physical DNA. You can change your name, be disowned by your parents, deny your identity, act in ways that are unbecoming, make foolish choices, or whatever, but you will never lose the DNA you received at birth.

When you were born the second time (born from above) you received DNA that comes from divine genetics. This is exactly what Paul is saying in the verse you just read. When you accepted Christ, you became a new person. That's right. Your old life is gone, and your new life has begun. There's been an exchange of genetics. The new you bears the DNA of your heavenly Father. There is absolutely nothing you can do that will cause you to lose your spiritual DNA. The Father will always treat you like his child because that's who you are—even when you don't act like a child of God. You can't lose with your bad works what you did not get with your good works. As God's child, you bear his divine nature (2 Peter 1:4 NKJV).

## New Creation Thinking

One of the greatest struggles we have as believers is with new *creation thinking*. Because we don't have a healthy understanding of who we are in Christ, we are robbed of so many of our birthright privileges. We know our sins have been forgiven (we hope), and we're pretty sure we're going to heaven when we die, but that's about it. If you are absolutely settled in your understanding that your sins have been forgiven—past, present, and future—and that you have confidence that you're going to heaven when you die, you are way ahead of most Christians. When push comes to shove, the majority of believers can't say with certainty that they are unconditionally loved and accepted by God. They hope they are, but they have no confidence that they are.

The two sons in the Luke 15 parable provide us with some deep insights into what most of us wonder about: What does God think about us? How does God see us? How does God feel about us. The youngest son found it hard to live like a son because he *thought* like a slave. The oldest son had difficulty thinking like a son because he *lived* like a slave. Sound familiar? If we can solve our thinking problem, we can radically affect our behavior problem. We behave wrong because we think wrong. If we refuse to change our thinking, we will always recycle our experiences.

Now that we are new creations in Christ, we need to come to grips with new creation thinking. God's Word tells us that we have the mind of Christ (1 Corinthians 2:16 NLTV). When we begin to bring our thoughts into alignment with our identities in Christ, we become free indeed (John 8:36 NLTV).

## My Prayer for you

I pray that everyone who reads this book will have their understanding enlightened about their new creation identities. Father, you have given us the spirit of truth. You know everything about everything, and you have promised to teach us all things. Reveal to us who we are in you, how you feel about us, how you see us, and what you think about us—in Jesus's name.

# CHAPTER  ONE

# THREE STORIES, ONE PARABLE

---

## The Sheep, the Silver, and the Sons

It was not unusual to find Jesus surrounded by a spellbound audience. After all, he was the Master Teacher. Jesus could draw a crowd at the drop of a hat, and he would drop the hat if he had to. On this particular day, his audience consisted of tax collectors, who were considered the lowest of the low. Luke refers to the others in the crowd as "well-known sinners." The crowd that had gathered to hear Jesus this day were legitimate card-carrying sinners. The outcast and rejected of society were drawn to Jesus like a moth to a lamp. It was common to see the down-and-outs huddled around Jesus. They instinctively knew there was something different about this man and in what he taught. They felt at ease and comfortable in his presence.

There were also some up-and-outs in the crowd that day: religious leaders from the synagogue called Pharisees. They were standing within earshot and could hear what Jesus was saying. Sprinkled among the Pharisees were some scribes. These scribes were teachers of the law. Both groups were expressing their dissatisfaction and annoyance that Jesus was meeting with sinners. In addition to this, he had the unmitigated gall to eat with these sinners. To eat with someone during that time in history and culture meant you accepted them. This was unacceptable to the religious hierarchy. These self-righteous Pharisees and scribes with their holier-than-thou attitudes were complaining about who Jesus was associating with. So Jesus spoke this parable to them (Luke 15:3 NKJV). The target audience for this parable were the religious elites.

Do we have three parables in Luke 15, or do we have three stories and one parable? I'm convinced we have one parable with three stories (windows), giving us the advantage of seeing the same truth from three different perspectives:

- What does God think about us?
- How does God see us?
- How does God feel about us?

The purpose behind this parable is to reveal the heart of the Father toward humanity.

## The Sheep

The parable began like this:

> A man had one hundred sheep, and he lost one.
> (Luke 15:4 NKJV)

This parable is about one out of one hundred. Instead of saying, "At least I still have ninety-nine sheep," the man left the ones he still had and went to search for the sheep that was lost. When he found the lost sheep, he placed it on his shoulders and brought it back to where it belonged. The sheep expended no effort whatsoever in being returned to its rightful place. The sheep had to be aware it was lost (out of place), but it did not know how to return to where it belonged.

Once the sheep owner returned with the sheep that had been out of place, he didn't scold or beat the sheep for wandering off, place it in quarantine to teach it a lesson, or put a shock collar around its neck; instead, he called his friends and neighbors over for a celebration. The invitation may have read something like this: "I've found my sheep that was lost. It is back where it belongs. Come join me in celebrating its return. It's time to have a party."

Jesus replied without hesitating:

> I say to you that likewise there will be more joy in heaven over one sinner who repents than over ninety-nine just persons who need no repentance. (Luke 15:7 NKJV)

Was Jesus really talking about a four-footed animal in this story? On many occasions, Jesus referred to his followers as sheep:

> My sheep hear My voice, and I know them, and they follow Me. And I give them eternal life, and they shall never perish; neither shall anyone snatch them out of My hand. My Father who has given them to Me, is greater than all; and no one is able to snatch them out of My Father's hand. I and My Father are one. (John 10:27–30 NKJV)

There is good reason to believe that Jesus wasn't talking about sheep in the first story. Could he be talking about people who are spiritually out of place, people who are not where they need to be?

## The Silver

After Jesus finished his short story about the lost sheep, he immediately began talking about a woman who had ten pieces of silver and lost one of them. This parable is about one in ten. Jesus went from talking about sheep to talking about silver. Like the man who had a burden to find his lost sheep, this woman was bent on finding her lost piece of silver. This woman could have said, "At least I still have nine pieces of silver." The one lost coin was on her mind, and she was determined to find it. She lit a lamp so she could see into every crack and crevice in her search for the lost coin. She took a broom and swept the entire house in her search for the out-of-place piece of silver. She didn't stop the search until she found it.

When the woman found the coin, she invited her friends and neighbors over for a celebration. "I've found the lost piece of silver. I would love for you to come to my house and celebrate with me." Her invitation could have read, "It's time to party!" I wonder if Jesus was really talking about silver coins:

> Likewise, I say to you, there is joy in the presence
> of the angels of God over one sinner who repents.
> (Luke 15:10 NKJV)

I don't think Jesus had a woman and her coin collection on his mind. He was talking about the importance and value of one lost soul.

The silver coin was out of place, but it didn't know it. What does a piece of silver know? Since it didn't know it was out of place, why would it have a desire to be back with the other nine pieces of silver? Maybe Jesus wasn't talking about silver at all. Is it possible that Jesus was talking about people who have no idea they're not where they need to be spiritually? How can a person get back in place if they don't know they're out of place? The search for the lost piece of silver was initiated by the woman. The coin had nothing to do with being placed back where it belonged.

## The Sons

Jesus continued telling his story without pausing: "A certain man had two sons" (Luke 15:11 NKJV). We have gone from sheep to silver to sons. The rate has gone from one in one hundred to one in ten—and now it's one in two. There's one thing we know for certain now; Jesus was not talking about four-footed animals or silver. He was talking about people: the father and his two sons.

The youngest of his two sons made an unwise decision. He decided to leave his father and strike out on his own. There was a big wild world out there, and he was determined to go tame it. This young man was going to discover that real freedom was found in submission to his father and not in rebellion against his father. Freedom without restraints is actually a baited trap that leads to bondage. He was on the verge of finding out that sin will take you further than you ever thought you would go, it will keep you there longer than you ever intended to stay, and it will cost you more than you ever expected to pay. Payday may not be every Friday, but there will always be a payday.

The youngest son did come to his senses and returned home. His father received him with open arms and loved him unconditionally. He was restored to his rightful place as a son. Just like the man who found his lost sheep and the woman who found her lost piece of silver, the father invited his neighbors to his home for a celebration. It was time to party.

The oldest son stayed home and continued to work for his father, but his heart had left home long before his youngest brother ever did. He shared his father's home, but he did not share his father's heart. We'll talk about this walkaway son in chapter 6.

## One Parable, Three Stories

There is one common thread that ties all three of these stories together. It is the celebration that takes place after that which was lost is recovered and returned to its rightful place. The man with the lost sheep, the woman with the lost silver, and the father with the lost boy had parties to celebrate what had been lost. All who were out of place were back where they belonged.

The intended audience for this parable was the Pharisees and the scribes (Luke 15:3 NKJV). The tax collectors and notorious sinners certainly heard it too. Jesus said, "What man of you?" (Luke 15:4 NKJV). Jesus told the story about the sheep that was missing. As soon as he finished, he said, "Or what woman?" (Luke 15:8 NKJV). He also talked about the woman who had lost the piece of silver. Without pausing, he said, "A certain man had two sons" (Luke 15:11 NKJV). It seems to me that Jesus used these three short stories to present one parable. He wanted both groups—the down-and-out and the up-and-out—to know what God thought about them, how he saw them, and how he felt about them. If you have a desire to know, all you have to do is pay attention to the attitude and actions the man, the woman, and the father had for what they had lost.

## Lost Soul

Jesus told another story about a lost soul. He went from talking about a lost sheep to a lost piece of silver to a lost son and then to a lost soul. This story is found in Luke 16:19–32 (NKJV). I don't think this is a parable because Jesus used a proper name in the story. He never used a person's name in any of the parables he told. He only used labels: the sower, the father, the prodigal son, the debtor, or the master. There is another distinction between this story and the other three. There is no celebration at the end because a lost soul (the soul that is out of place) is lost forever.

## Perspectives

> [God] Who desires all men to be saved and to come to the knowledge of the truth. (1 Timothy 2:4 JKJV)

We do know one thing about the Father's heart: he does not want to see anyone experience the rich man's fate in Luke 16. Over the years, I've heard people say, "If your God is so loving, why does he send people to hell?" God has never sent—nor will he ever send—anyone to hell. A person goes to hell because of their own choice: the choice not to accept Christ as their Lord and Savior. The rich man did not go to hell because of his material possessions. He went to hell because of his spiritual lack. Lazarus did not go to heaven because he was poor. He went to heaven because the Father knew his name, and he knew the Father:

> I am the good shepherd; and *I know My sheep* and am *known by My own.* (John 10:14 NKJV; emphasis added)

If you were driving down a familiar highway and began to see signs that told you to stop and turn around because the bridge was out, you would have a choice to make. You could obey the signs and turn around or ignore the signs and keep driving. You have no one to blame if you ignore the warning signs and crash and burn. It would be ludicrous to blame the people who posted the signs for your crash because you chose to ignore the warning.

## The Sheep's Perspective

We know now that Jesus was not talking about literal sheep. He was talking about people who have gone astray because they have been focused only on their needs. Their free grazing has led them astray. Their self-centeredness has led to them to wander aimlessly away from where they needed to be. They know they are out of place and need to return to the "flock of faith," but they don't know how.

The sheep was not looking for the shepherd, but the shepherd was looking for the sheep. God is always the pursuer of that which is lost. After Adam and Eve disobeyed God, they hid themselves because they were afraid. How in the world can you hide from God if he is everywhere at the same time? It's insane, but that's how the unredeemed mind thinks. The idea that God is the pursuer for that which is out of place has its genesis in chapter 3 in the book of beginnings (Genesis 3:8 NKJV).

What does God think about this one lost sheep? How does he see it? How does he feel about it? If he's willing to leave the ninety-nine to go search for it, it must be of value to him. He didn't drive it back to the herd when he found it. He carried it on his shoulders. The lost sheep made no contribution to being placed back where it belonged. The effort was solely on the part of the shepherd.

## The Silver's Perspective

Was Jesus talking about a piece of silver that was missing from a woman's coin collection or a person who is not where they need to be spiritually? I think we know he's talking about a person.

There are people who are out of place, but unlike the sheep, they don't know it. How can a piece of silver return to where it belongs if it doesn't know it's out of place? What does a piece of silver know anyway? The piece of silver was not looking for the woman, but the woman was looking for the piece of silver. She kept searching until she found it. Once the coin was found, she placed it back where it belonged. Just like the sheep, it had nothing to do with being restored to its rightful place. It was all the woman's doing. She sought it, she found it, and she restored it:

For the Son of Man (Jesus) has come to seek and to
save that which was lost. (Luke 19:10 NKJV)

The party was on when she found it. Why? Because the coin was
valuable to her. It had worth.

## The Son's Perspective

The son knew he was out of place. He also knew what to do about
it. However, he wrestled with a big question: "Would he be accepted
or allowed to come home?" This was his biggest concern. He was
not sure how his father would react to him coming back to where he
belonged. The boy made a bad choice with his life, and he felt like
he was no longer worthy of being called a son (Luke 15:19 NKJV).
He would settle for being a slave. It's hard to live like a son if you
think like a slave.

When the boy was still a long distance away, the father saw him
coming. This tells us the father was looking for his son to return.
The father ran to his son, grabbed him in his arms, and loved on
him. He was received with joy and accepted unconditionally (Luke
15:20 NKJV). Surely the boy had a slight odor. He had just left the
pigpen. The smell of swine could not snuff out the love the father
had for his boy. There was more grace in the father's heart than there
was sin in his son.

Even though the son would have settled with being a slave in his
father's house, he was treated like a son. That was the only way the
father could treat him. Why? Because he was his son. He was out
of place (lost), but he went back to where he belonged. It was time
to celebrate—and celebrate they did. The father's thoughts about
his son, the way he saw his son, and how he felt about his son was
revealed by the way he treated his son when he came home. The
prodigal son found grace in his father's home because grace was in
his father's heart.

*Wayne Kniffen*

## Is Jesus Telling Our Story?

I have a suspicion that all of us can relate to the sheep, the silver, or the sons in some form or fashion. It's possible to get so engrossed with our own grazing that we wander away from the place we belong—only to find ourselves alone and in need of rescue. The grass just over the hill always looks a little greener. If this describes you, stop wandering and start watching for the Shepherd. He is on his way. He is looking for you.

You may be like the piece of silver that was lost and didn't know it. If you don't know you're out of place, there's no desire to be back in place. This is a very dangerous place to be because it has eternal consequences. If the expression "being lost" sounds alien or weird to you, you have just read your first warning sign: "Stop and turn around—the bridge is out!" You have no one to blame but yourself if you crash and burn. Go back and read the story about the lost soul in Luke 16. Unlike the sheep, the silver, and the son, the lost soul is lost forever. There will be no celebration.

You may not be able to relate to the lost sheep or the lost silver, but you do have an affinity to the son who willfully removed himself from his father's authority. He wrote a check with his mouth that his life couldn't cash. This young man felt he was missing out on life. He began to imagine a life without restraints. He wanted to be free to follow the call of the wild. These uncaptured thoughts led him to make a bad decision. He got sucker punched by bondage disguised as freedom. The lures of this world are attractive, seductive, and enticing. If you take the bite, you may be hooked for life.

The prodigal son had a come-to-the-father moment when he was in the pen with the pigs. He came to his senses. For the first time, he realized he had swapped his swag for swine. It was in that defining moment that he came to his senses. That means he left his senses when he walked away from his father. He came back to the same father he walked away from—a father filled with love and grace.

## Focus on the Father

It is so easy to get distracted by small things and miss the main thing. We can learn a lot about what the Father thinks about us, how he sees us, and how he feels about us by looking at how the silver, the sheep, and the sons were treated. However, the most important thing is keeping the main thing the main thing—our focus should be on the Father.

You are the apple of your Father's eyes, and there are no worms in his apples: "I will never leave you nor forsake you" (Hebrews 13:5 NKJV). The writer of Hebrews borrowed these words from Deuteronomy 31. With incredible simplicity, this verse reveals the heart of the Father. In this passage, God is saying that his heart is always focused on you. He will never turn his heart away from you. Our heavenly Father loves us today, when we are lovable, and he will love us tomorrow, when we are unlovable. He will love us even if we wander away like sheep, find ourselves out of place like the piece of silver, or make a bad decision like the prodigal son. He will never turn his heart away from us.

Many years ago, Mike Payne and Ronny Hinson cowrote "When He Was on the Cross." This incredible song encapsulates the very heart of God:

> He knew me, yet he loved me
> He whose glory makes the heavens shine
> So unworthy of such mercy
> Yet when he was on the cross
> I was on his mind.

Since God is our Creator, he knows us better than we know ourselves—yet he still loves us. We're so unworthy of his mercy, yet when he was dying on the cross, we were on his mind. This answers the questions unequivocally: What does God think about you? How does God see you? How does God feel about you? You are always in his heart and on his mind.

CHAPTER  TWO

# THE RUNAWAY

---

he big day had finally arrived. The youngest of the two sons was about to act on what he'd been thinking about. He'd been dreaming for some time about what life would be like without restraints. He had convinced himself that the only way he could be happy was to have a life without boundaries—free from all restrictions. Uncaptured thoughts produce runaway feelings. This young man was about to make a decision that would have severe consequences based on feelings that had convinced him they were reality.

This is a great illustration why the Word of God tells us to capture our thoughts and bring them into captivity (2 Corinthians 10:5 NKJV). Thoughts left to run wild have the ability to paint pictures of what appears to be reality but is only a facade. Reality is whatever God says. Whenever we allow our thoughts to move us away from what God says, we are no longer living in reality. This young man didn't know it, but he was on his way to having a reality check. It was just a matter of time. Always remember this about time: Time will either indict you or vindicate you. Just give it time.

## The Runaway's Demand

> The younger son told his father, "I want my share of
> your estate now before you die." (Luke 15:12 NLTV)

It is hard to believe that anyone could be this cold and insensitive, especially to someone who loves them unconditionally and has sacrificed to make sure they are well provided for. This is absolutely jaw-dropping.

There is something very important in this one-way conversation that is taking place between the father and his son—and we need to pay attention to it. The father did not try to talk him out of his decision to leave home. It was not because the father did not know what would be lurking in the shadows of the faraway country that could destroy his son or because he did not know his son. He was well aware that his son lacked the maturity and discipline to survive in a dog-eat-dog world.

It is so easy to get caught up in the stories that Jesus tells and forget what he is doing. We need to remind ourselves again that this is a parable. It is an earthy story that has a heavenly meaning. This is our story. God has given us a free will, and he will never infringe on it—not even if we are in the process of making bad decisions. The father in this parable did not try to talk his son out of leaving home.

I'm sure the father was grieved to hear his son talking this way. He loved his boy, and he knew how cruel the world could be, especially to the naïve:

> So his father agreed to divide his wealth between
> his sons. (Luke 15:12 NLTV)

Pay attention to what the father did. He divided his wealth between his sons. Both sons were given their share of their father's estate. This will have more significance when we talk about the eldest son, the walkaway, in chapter 6.

## The Day of Departure

A few days later, the father's youngest son packed his bag and left home. He took his first step as a free man. Ah! A life with no boundaries and no authority figures telling you what you can or cannot do. It was a dream come true. Dressed for the occasion, he was on his way to living the good life, a life of his own choosing.

As he walked along, looking cool and smelling good, I can see him occasionally patting the money pouch that was strapped around his waist. The money bag was as full as he was of himself. It never crossed his mind that both would end up empty. Life was good, and it was going to get better. Look out world—here comes the man! He had his swag on.

It didn't take long to get to the faraway country. It actually was only a thought away. Just because a person doesn't leave home physically, it doesn't mean they haven't left home. It's possible to be physically present and mentally absent at the same time. I'm sure he was bug-eyed when the lights of the faraway country came into view. Thinking about all the possibilities that were at his fingertips must have caused his heart to pound in his chest. Everything he had been thinking about was becoming a reality.

Self-discipline comes from mastering your thoughts. If you're unable to control what you think, you will not be able to control what you do. This boy was now out of place—just like the sheep and the piece of silver were. What got him out of place was his thought life. He had not mastered his thoughts, and he was unable to control his actions. Thoughts produce feelings, and feelings determine behavior. If we think wrong, it's just a matter of time before we start behaving wrong. If we believe right, we will behave right. When you see someone behaving wrong, you are seeing someone who has a thinking problem.

## The Cost of Wild Living

It didn't long before the young man had wasted all his money on wild living (Luke 15:13 NLTV). Jesus did not define wild living for us. He didn't have to. Our imaginations can do that for us. The bag that had been bulging with money when he left home was empty. It was as empty as his life. The young man was on the verge of discovering that all play days have a payday. You play—you pay.

Where were all the friends he had made? As long as you are the one buying the drinks, you are the man of the hour. I'm sure he was surrounded by a crowd of partiers who were more than eager to sing his praises: "For he's a jolly good fellow that nobody can deny." I wonder where all the beautiful women were who had been hanging on his arm and whispering in his ear. Bondage disguised as freedom was beginning to close its grip on the young man. We have the freedom to make choices, but we are not free from the consequences of our choices.

The father knew the day would eventually come, but he did not try to talk his son out of leaving home. Sometimes true love will let you learn a lesson the hard way:

> And He gave them their request, But sent leanness into their souls. (Psalm 106:15 NKJV)

Sometimes, the worst thing that can happen to us is getting what we think we want. Some things are easier to get your hands on than they are to turn loose.

## Lessons We Can Learn from the Boy's Mistakes

The best lessons often come from our own mistakes. We can all learn from our mistakes, but the truly wise person learns from the mistakes of others. Tom Bodett said, "In school, you're taught a lesson and then given a test. In life, you're given a test that teaches you a lesson." Sin has the ability to make us look foolish—so that we can only learn the hard way.

One of the best lessons we can learn from this young man's mistakes is the importance of maintaining a healthy thought life. We must guard our thoughts at all costs. Thoughts are not just benign flashes going off in our heads. Thoughts are creative and filled with potential that can be positive or negative if spoken or acted upon. A thought can't live unless it is spoken. This is why we should be quick to hear but slow to speak (James 1:19 NKJV). This young man's thoughts had been painting pictures of a life without restraints or restrictions in his head for a long time. His thoughts had convinced him that the only way he would ever be happy was to be out from under his father's authority. Zig Ziglar said, "What consumes your mind controls your life."

How we live our lives on a daily basis is predicated upon our thought lives. We will ultimately act on what we have been thinking about. The father's young son had been thinking about leaving home for a long time. His thoughts were continually fixed on the faraway country. He thought about it so much that he could see the bright lights of the city in his mind's eye. He could hear the sounds of the party life, the music, and the dancing. The smell of independence was intoxicating. The only thing it would take for his thoughts to become reality would be the right moment. The enemy of our souls will always make sure that happens. If this young man had captured his thoughts and weighed them on the scales of truth, he would have made a different decision. Wacky thoughts of living life without restrictions fed his flesh, and the flesh has never enjoyed being told what it can or cannot do.

Another life-changing lesson we can learn from this young man has to do with free will. Because we have the gift of free choice, our heavenly Father will never usurp control over the decisions we make. The Holy Spirit may tug on our heartstrings to get us to slow down so we can examine what we are about to do. He may give us some promptings, but ultimately, he will allow us to decide what we are going to do. He will not take over and make decisions for us. Having free will keeps us from being human robots. The father did not argue with his son when he demanded his share of the family estate. He did not try to convince him that he was making a bad decision to move to the faraway country. The son had his mind set on what he was going to do, and his father was not going to override his free will—even though he knew the decision he was making would have severe consequences.

The gift of free will removes any and all guilt transference for our bad decisions. Free will takes away the blame game. We cannot blame God for not talking us out of the bad choices we have made or will make. As a new creation being, we have the mind of Christ (1 Corinthians 2:16 NKJV). If this is true, and I'm convinced it is, we have the ability to capture our thoughts and make healthy choices in life.

Sometimes the best degree that can be earned comes from the University of Hard Knocks. The father's youngest son graduated summa cum laude. We might say he graduated "come soon, Lord." The biggest mistake this young man made was removing himself from his father's covering. There is no freedom apart from the Father's covering. True freedom has boundaries. Real freedom has restrictions and limitations. Without them, all you have is bondage cloaked in the garments of freedom. The enemy is a formable foe. He is skilled at concealing the truth. God, on the other hand, reveals the truth.

This story Jesus is telling is about *us*. It is so easy to get caught up in the story's plot and forget that Jesus is talking about us and our heavenly Father: what he thinks about us, how he sees us, and how he feels about us. Everything the human heart cries out for can only be found in the Father. The Word of God says that Christ is our life (Colossians 3:4 NKJV). Without him, we have no real life. Paul said, "For in Him (Jesus) we live and move and having or being" (Acts 17:28 NKJV). Without Christ, we would be forever stuck in the faraway country— and we would be destitute.

## Things Can Go from Bad to Worse

"When he had spent all" (Luke 15:14 NKJV). These five words tell the whole story about sinful living. Sin will cost you far more than you think you will have to pay. The seed of his rebellion against his father's authority was producing fruit. He was left with an empty money pouch, hollow dreams, a meaningless life, and unfilled expectations. His entire being was lacking substance, meaning, and value.

This once-well-dressed young man once had the world by the tail, and then he was crouching in an alley in the faraway country, looking like a vacuous vagabond, with no hope of life getting any better. The sad commentary about this young man's condition is that it was avoidable. He planted a thought, which led to a word, and then an action, which produced a habit, which developed his character, and then he was reaping his destiny. He had spent all!

It is easy to overlook that he was still a son. He might have been living like a slave, and he might not have looked as good as a slave, but he was still a son. This was the father's son who was out of place by choice. He was lost—just like the sheep and the piece of silver Jesus talked about. Was there any hope for him? Surely, he had gone too far and committed too much sin to be called a child of the father. What did the father think about his son then? How do you think the father saw him? How do you think the father felt about his son?

This is where the rubber meets the road. How does God see us when we make choices that have ruinous consequences? Surely, he can't love us as much as he did before we messed up so badly. How can his feelings toward us be the same as they once were since we've disappointed him so much?

Here is some good news. We can never disappoint God because it is impossible for us to do anything He did not know we would do. All the poor choices that we make in life never abate His love for us. Poor choices will prevent us from enjoying our birthright privileges. God is love.

The father knew what would happen to his son when he chose to move to the faraway country, yet he did not try to convince him not to leave. The father was not going to violate his son's freedom to choose. Freedom of choice is what separates us from all other life forms. We are where we are today because of the choices we made yesterday. Where we will be tomorrow will be determined by the choices we make today. It would behoove all of us to make capturing our thoughts a priority.

The youngest son was hunkered down in an alley in the far county because of the choice he made when he lived in his father's home. It's a crying shame when humanity finds sheltering in the alleys of this world a better option than finding shelter in the home of the Father. The reason most people do is because they do not feel like they will be welcomed by the Father. The devil has whispered this lie in the ears of the prodigals of this world, and they believe it. Here is what Jesus said about the devil:

> You are of your father the devil, and the desires of your father you want to do. He was a murderer from the beginning, and does not stand in the truth, because there is no truth in him. When he speaks a lie, he speaks from his own resources, for he is a liar and the father of it. (John 8:44 NKJV)

Pay attention to the words that follow:

> When he had spent all, there arose a severe famine in that land, and he began to be in want. (Luke 15:14 NKJV)

Things had gone from bad to worse. Some people say, "Cheer up because things can get worse." Well, things can get worse—and they did for this young man. The famine that hit the land only magnified the famine he was experiencing inside of himself. It's a tough gig when a person's physical condition becomes as empty as their spiritual condition.

Sometimes the best place we can come to is the end of ourselves. It gives us an advantage point where we can assess where we are, how we got here, and what we can do to get to where we need to be. Have you ever thought that being at the end of your rope is an advantage point? When I was a young preacher, a man I deeply respected, John H. Beard, said, "When you get to the end of your rope, tie a prayer knot and hold on." Holding on may be the hardest thing a person can do.

I doubt very seriously this young man ever dreamed his life would end up this way. He thought he knew what he wanted in life, but ending up in want was not part of it. Everything he left home with was gone, including his swag. All those uncaptured thoughts that were allowed to run unchallenged in this young man's head had taken their toll. He had spent it all.

## Poor Planning

The prodigal son never had tomorrow on his mind. He was totally focused on living by the seat of his pants—today. If you get caught up with living by the flesh today, tomorrow never crosses you mind. The choices we make today without considering tomorrow can create situations that will jerk us around like a yo-yo on a string. The prodigal son ended up in the pigsty because he left God out of his plans (James 4:13–15 NKJV). He was the victim of his own poor planning.

On December 4, 1958, in his Oxford Union address, Gerard Hoffnung shared a made-up story about a professional bricklayer. It was his response to his worker's compensation claim for injuries sustained on the job. It seems the insurer sought more detailed information for their accident investigation about how the bricklayer sustained such substantial injuries.

Dear sir:

I am writing in response to your request for additional information in block 3 of the accident report form. I put "poor planning" as the cause of my accident. You asked for a fuller explanation, and I trust the following details will be sufficient.

I am a bricklayer by trade. On the day of the accident, I was working alone on the roof of a new six-story building. When I completed my work, I found I had some bricks left over, which, when weighed later, were found to be slightly in excess of five hundred pounds. Rather than carry the bricks down by hand, I decided to lower them in a barrel by using a pulley, which was attached to the side of the building on the sixth floor.

Securing the rope at the ground level, I went up to the roof, swung the barrel out, and loaded the bricks into it. Then I went down and untied the rope, holding it tightly to ensure a slow descent of the bricks. You will note in block 11 of the accident report form that I weigh 135 pounds.

Due to my surprise at being jerked off the ground so suddenly, I lost my presence of mind and forgot to let go of the rope. Needless to say, I proceeded at a rapid rate up the side of the building. In the vicinity of the third floor, I met the barrel, which was now proceeding downward at an equally impressive speed. This explains the fractured skull, minor abrasions, and the broken collarbone, as listed in section 3 of the accident report.

Slowed only slightly, I continued my rapid ascent, not stopping until the fingers of my right hand were two knuckles deep into the pulley.

Fortunately, by this time, I had regained my presence of mind and was able to hold tightly to the rope, in spite of the excruciating pain I was now beginning to experience. At approximately the same time, however, the barrel of bricks hit the ground and the bottom fell out of the barrel. Now devoid of the weight of the bricks, that barrel weighed approximately fifty pounds. I refer you again to my weight of 135 pounds.

As you might imagine, I began a rapid descent, down the side of the building. In the vicinity of the third floor, I met the barrel coming up. This accounts for the two fractured ankles, broken tooth, and severe lacerations of my legs and lower body. Here my luck began to change slightly. The encounter with the barrel seemed to slow me enough to lessen my injuries when I fell into the pile of bricks, and fortunately only three vertebrae were cracked.

I am sorry to report, however, as I lay there on the pile of bricks, in pain, unable to move, I again lost my composure and presence of mind and let go of the rope, and I lay there watching the empty barrel begin its journey back down onto me. This explains the two broken bones.

I hope this answers your inquiry as to my "poor planning."

Life has a way of jerking us around and rendering us senseless at times. Battered, bruised, and broken, we limp around and try to make sense out of nonsense. When this happens, don't run from the Father—run *to* him. Our bad choices in life have not changed him one iota. "He is the same yesterday, today, and forever" (Hebrews 13:8 NKJV). God's love for us never fails (Psalm 136:1 NLTV).

# CHAPTER THREE

# PIGPEN RESOLUTION

---

## From Swag to Swine

When our lives spiral out of control, we may find ourselves doing things we said we would never do or think we would ever do. The following words may have a familiar ring to them because they have been spoken by the vast majority of humanity: "You will never catch me doing that. I will never _____." You can fill in the blank. It is easy to say what you will or will never do if you have never worn the shoes of the person who has.

This young man is desperate, and he has lost everything:

> He persuaded a local farmer to hire him, and the man sent him into his fields *to feed the pigs*. (Luke 15:15 NLTV; emphasis added)

Let me interject something before moving on. There is one thing this boy has not lost; he has not lost his father who loves him unconditionally. He is going to find this out one day—but not this day. He has not been broken enough. God will use the swine to root out his remaining swag.

You know things have gotten bad when corn husks and pig slop look good to you. That's exactly what happened:

> The young man became so hungry that even the pods he was feeding the pigs looked good to him. *But no one gave him anything.* (Luke 15:16 NLTV; emphasis added)

The world does not have what a person needs when they find themselves out of place, which was why no one gave him anything. The world cannot put anyone back where they belong. The world's system can never satisfy the hunger of a lost soul. What this boy needed could only be found in the arms of his father. The world, with all of its attractions, can never quench the thirst of a parched soul. It may give the appearance that it can, but that's all it is: an appearance.

## A Come-to-Jesus Moment

"When he finally came to his senses" (Luke 15:17 NLTV). Before this pigpen moment, this young man was not in his right mind. His come-to-Jesus experience happened while he was in the pen with the pigs. All of a sudden, his mind began to clear—and reality started to kick in. He was having a moment where reasonable and rational thinking were beginning to return. Poor judgment was beginning to fade, and it was slowly being replaced by sound reasoning. Sometimes it takes a pigpen experience to get our undivided attention. Living in a pen with pigs doesn't make you a pig, but you will certainly smell like one.

I remember my pigpen resolution moment as if it happened yesterday. It took place in Vietnam in 1968. My illusion of being invincible had been shattered. The reality of death, pain, and suffering had exposed my spiritual lostness. I was that lost sheep

Jesus talked about. I was that out-of-place piece of silver the woman was searching for. My choices had finally painted me into a corner. My options were limited. I could keep running, which would have led to further misery, or I could stop, throw up my hands, and surrender to the Father. Running to my heavenly Father was the best decision I have ever made.

I discovered that God was not mad at me. He welcomed me with open arms and showered me with his unconditional love. He didn't lecture me or scold me. He lovingly began to show me what he thought about me, how he saw me, and how he felt about me. I can give a personal testimony to what a blessing it can be to find yourself in a pen with pigs, having spent all, and no one giving you anything.

## The Prodigal Has Another Talk with Himself

For the first time in a long time, this young man began to think about home. The draw wasn't the material things that were available in his father's house. The magnet pulling on his heartstrings was his father.

Can you imagine how many people are hiding in alleys and on the backstreets of far countries in this world, who desperately need to come home, but believe they will be rejected by the Father if they return. They know where they belong, but they don't think they will be welcomed. Let me give you some good news. You may have wasted your substance and livelihood, but you have not lost the love your heavenly Father has for you. He is waiting for you with open arms to receive and restore you. He is ready to celebrate your homecoming:

> When he finally came to his senses, he said to himself, "At home even the hired servants have food enough to spare, and here I am dying of hunger." (Luke 15:17 NLTV)

This out-of-place young man begins to think about how well his father takes care of his servants. The servants in his father's house have more than enough provision. They are living comfortably inside a beautiful home with all its amenities while he lives outside in a pigsty. The servants are faring well, but the son cannot get on welfare.

This prodigal started having a very serious conversation with himself. Having an honest talk with oneself can be the most productive thing one can do. I think he was ready to listen. His self-talk was what got him in trouble in the first place. His thoughts had convinced him that he would be happier and freer living life out from under his father's roof and authority. That really turned out to be wrong! True freedom is not casting all caution to the wind. Freedom has boundaries and restrictions. If you violate these perimeters, you will end up anything but free:

> I will arise and go to my father and will say to him, "Father, I have sinned against heaven and before you, and *I am no longer worthy to be called your son. Make me like one of your hired servants.*" (Luke 15:18–19 NKJV; emphasis added)

This is the resolution he made while he was in the pigpen: "I will return home to my father." This decision was probably harder to make than the one he made to leave home.

Let's put ourselves in the head of this young man and listen to the conversation he was having with himself: *If I stay where I am, the end results will be my demise. I can't keep going the way I'm going. These pigs have less concern about their survival than I do. They are freer than I am. This certainly has not turned out the way I thought it would. I've made a huge mistake, and I'm not sure my father will allow me to come home. But going home is my only option if I am to survive.*

*I know my father has to be disappointed in me. I wonder what he*

*thinks about me now. How will he see me? How will he feel about me?*
*I have brought so much reproach upon him and his name. I'll tell him*
*that I realize I have sinned against heaven and against him. I also know*
*there's a good chance he may not receive me back as his son, so I will ask*
*him to make me one of his servants. I know one thing—if he will take*
*me back as a servant, I'll live better in his home as a servant than I'm*
*living in this faraway country as his son.*

One of the main reasons why believers have a difficult time
coming back to where they belong is because they think they have
disappointed God so much that he may refuse to accept them.
Is it possible for us to disappoint God? Most Christians believe
we can. For us to be able to disappoint God, we would have to
do something that he didn't know or expect us to do. Since he is
all-knowing (omniscient), disappointing him is impossible. If we
could do something that he didn't know we would do, then he
would not be all-knowing. We can grieve the Holy Spirit, resist
the Holy Spirit, offend the Holy Spirit, insult the Holy Spirit, and
quench the Holy Spirit, but we can never disappoint God. This is
good news.

When he came to his senses, this young man got to his feet, set
his sights in the direction of his father's home, and struck out. I bet
his walk home was at a much slower gait than it was when he left
home.

## It's Hard to Live like a Son If You Think like a Slave

This young man sure had a different mindset going home than he
did when he left home. He was not as full of himself as he was when
he walked away. I would lay odds that he no longer had his money
pouch either. We know for certain that he had no sandals. He either
lost his shoes or hocked them at the local pawnshop. I'm guessing
he did the latter.

Try to imagine what he looked like then to how he looked when he walked away from home. He was a living pictorial of the cost for low living. When he left home, he was dressed like a millionaire playboy, smelled good, and was running over with confidence. He now reeked with the smell of pigs, the cockiness and swag were gone, and his clothes were soiled and stained with the stench of the world. As bad as he looked on the outside, it could not compare to how bad he looked on the inside.

I'm sure there were moments during his walk home when he toyed with the idea of turning around. How could he face his father? He had written a huge check with his mouth that his life couldn't cash. He was so proud and pompous when he struck out for the faraway country. What a difference a brief period of time can make. Time had indicted him. He was going home like a whipped dog, and he smelled like one too.

He had the mindset of a king when he left home. He had the mindset of a slave on his way back home. It is hard to live like a son if you think like a slave.

This young man is a graphic illustration of what the world can and will do to a child of God who is determined to get their needs met by the world instead of by their heavenly Father. Allow the Holy Spirit to paint an indelible picture of this boy in your mind because you are seeing the fruit that comes from the tree of the knowledge of good and evil: getting one's needs met independent of God.

The siren call of the wild to live free is very seductive. Many sons and daughters have not been able to resist its promise of freedom— only to be abused, used, and then dumped like last week's rubbish.

To keep from becoming a statistic, you must keep thinking like a child of God. This does not come easily or happen naturally. It must be intentional. As long as we are in this world, there will be distractions. Dealing with distractions is not an option, but giving in to distractions is. It is hard to live like children of God if we think like slaves.

## Our Worthiness Comes from Who We Belong To—and Not from What We Do

In his conversation with himself, the prodigal said, "I will tell my father that I am not worthy to be called his son" (Luke 15:19). After disappointing himself, he thought his father would be disappointed in him as well. He didn't feel like a son, and he assumed his father would feel the same way.

Feelings of unworthiness are an Achilles' heel for most Christians. The world has convinced us that our worthiness comes from what we do: our performance. As long as we are successful, we feel good about ourselves. We have a sense of worth and value. When we are stumbling, our feelings of worth and value go down the tube. Being worthy has nothing to do with how we feel. Feelings are just that: feelings. Feelings come, and feelings go. There's only one thing consistent about feelings; they are forever changing. This is exactly where the enemy of our soul wants us to live: in the confines of our feelings. If we acquiesce to his scheme, we will spend our entire lives on an emotional roller coaster. Our lives will be filled with ups and downs and sudden extreme changes. Peace will be conspicuous by its absence in our lives.

Our worth is not determined by what we do or don't do. This is why the prodigal did not feel like he was worthy to be called a son. His perception of reality was based on his feelings. Feelings are not fundamental to faith, and if our feelings are allowed to be the judge of reality, we may believe something that is not real. Our worth is determined by our birth—and not by our behavior.

## Resolutions Don't Have to Take Place in a Pigsty

A come-to-the-Father moment can happen anyplace, anytime, anywhere. It does not have to take place in a pigsty in some faraway county. All we need is a come-to-our-senses moment wherever we find ourselves. It is possible to leave home mentally and emotionally and still be in the house physically. If home is where the heart is, then it's possible to be in the house and be at home somewhere else—wherever our heart may be.

"I will arise and go to my father" (Luke 15:18 NKJV). His first step in the wrong direction brought him to this place. He had taken the first step in the right direction. When he had a change of mind, he had a change of heart, which led to a change in direction. "I will go to my father." This was the best decision this young man had made in a long time.

The word *arise* is an interesting choice of words. This same word is used in regard to the resurrection of Jesus Christ from the dead. Jesus *arose* from an impossible situation that he brought upon himself by choice. He chose to take our place on the cross, suffer our penalty for sin, and die our death. Satan could not seduce him, Pilate could not kill him, and the grave could not hold him. On the third day, Jesus did the impossible—he arose. When he *arose*, he took the sting out of death and victory out of the grave for every child of God.

The prodigal found himself in a situation of his own choosing. He had no one to blame but himself for the condition he was in. Death was the next item on the agenda for his life. I seriously doubt that dying was on his bucket list when he walked away from his father. His decision to *arise* and return to his father kept him from certain death. His free will choice to return to his father was his moment of resurrection.

I could write a book about people who had their resurrection moment while living in the land of plenty. They never desired to leave home to go "find themselves." Wild living was never appealing or attractive to them. Surrendering their lives to Jesus Christ never crossed their minds. When they heard the good news of the Gospel, the Spirit of God brought them to the realization of their need for salvation. They made a resolution to accept and receive Jesus Christ as their personal Lord and Savior. It's not necessarily the place we find ourselves in that makes us a prodigal, it's the position and condition of our hearts. We can be in the right place physically and in the wrong place spiritually.

## Some Who Are Out of Place Don't Know They're Out of Place

Many years ago, I pastored a man who was an all-American kind of guy. He was highly ethical and had outstanding moral character. He was one of the best employees in his company. You could not have asked for a better husband, father, or family man. He was faithful in attending the services we had at our church facilities, and he was very generous with his resources. He had a passion to help those in need. You couldn't have asked for a better man or friend.

There was one thing missing in this man's life: he had never accepted or received Jesus Christ as his Lord and Savior. When we had our first discussion about personal intimacy with the Lord, I was taken aback when he told me he had never "done that." Without pressing him too hard, he told me how he had watched how Christians act for years. He felt the way he lived his life, in comparison to theirs, was just as good if not better. He wasn't being high-minded when he told me this. He was actually telling the truth.

Over an extended period of time and innumerable one-on-one times together, he came to realize his need to have a personal relationship with the Lord. He was like that out-of-place piece of silver Jesus talked about. He was out of place, but since he didn't know it, he had no desire to be where he belonged. Like the woman searching for the lost piece of silver, the Holy Spirit kept working on the inside of him searching with the light of truth. What a day that was when he prayed a simple prayer of faith and accepted Christ as his personal Lord and Savior.

He and I remained friends long after I left that church to go pastor in another city. It was a sad day, yet a sweet day, when I preached his celebration service. "Absent from the body, present with the Lord" is more than just a Bible verse my friend loved; it is now a living reality (2 Corinthians 5:8 NKJV). He is home with his Father. What a party that must have been!

## You Played—Now You Pay

A pastor friend called to see if he could spend some time with me. He wanted someone to know his life story. When we met, he poured out his soul. He did not hold back anything. His physical days were numbered, and he knew it. It would not be long before he transitioned to glory. I could tell my friend was not feeling well. The buildup of bilirubin in his blood had made him jaundiced. His skin and the whites of his eyes were yellow, he had lost a lot of weight, and his physical weakness was very noticeable.

For many years, he had been a chronic heroin user. He had spent the majority of his young adult life doing drugs in the slums of a large city in Texas. He shot up several times a day. He said he smoked it and snorted it, but his favorite way of administering the drug into his body was by injection. His heavy drug abuse had damaged his liver extensively. His liver could no longer efficiently process red blood cells as they broke down.

A well-known street evangelist brought the message of the Father's love to the streets and alleys of this large Texas town, witnessing and ministering to these prodigals. He understood their condition because he had been *one of them* too—a drug user and a gang leader. This man won thousands of these societal castaways to Jesus. One of his converts was the friend that I was talking to in the parking lot of the church where I pastored. He heard the good news about a loving, forgiving Father, came to his senses, got out of his pigpen, and experienced his resurrection. For the first time in his life, he was living.

Like the young man who had won him to Christ, he became a preacher of the grace of God. He pastored a small church in East

Texas. We became friends, and he felt like he could share his heart with me without being judged.

He told me to my face that he knew he was dying. He was well aware that he did not have much time left in this physical realm. He told me that he had no one to blame but himself. He had become a casualty of his own pathetic choices. He was not angry with God because he knew how the Holy Spirit had tried to get his attention on numerous occasions. My friend was hardheaded and would not listen. He lived under the delusion that he could handle his drug addiction by himself. He was well aware that he was experiencing the consequences of his own choices. My pastor friend chose to play, and now he was going to pay for it with his life.

Not long after our conversation, my friend made his transition from the earthly realm to the heavenly realm. Absent from the body, he was present with the Father.

We can never stray too far away in this earthly life to be out of the Father's reach. Our sinful spending cannot exhaust the Father's grace account. The Father yearns for you to come home. He is waiting to shower you with his unconditional love. The Father has no sermon to preach to you, no lecture to give, and no "I told you so." What he does have for you is mercy and grace. He is ready to celebrate your homecoming.

I can hear the Holy Spirit saying, "Arise and come home to the Father."

CHAPTER  FOUR

# THE FATHER'S HEART

---

## A Heart of Grace

The heart of this parable is about to be fully revealed. Jesus was telling this story in response to the complaints and criticism coming from the Pharisees and scribes because he was willing to spend time with the dregs of society. God sees worth in all of humanity. When it comes to human value, there are no favorites in the eyes of God. Jesus wants these religious leaders to know that the heart of the Father is for all of humanity to be restored to the place they belong (1 Timothy 2:4 NKJV). The religious crowd looked at and judged people through the eyes of their sanctimonious egos. The Father looks at people through the eyes of his heart—a heart of grace.

In this parable, Jesus talks about a man who had one hundred sheep. This man represents Jesus, the Good Shepherd. He is working on the outside, looking for the lost. One sheep ends up out of place. Even though it's only one, Jesus sees the worth and value of this one sheep. He leaves the ninety-nine and goes to search for the one that is lost.

Jesus talks about a woman who had ten pieces of silver. This woman represents the Holy Spirit. She is working on the inside searching with the light of truth for the one lost piece of silver.

The woman, just like the shepherd, knows the value and worth of this one piece of silver.

The father in this story represents the heavenly Father. He has a searching heart and is always on the lookout for out-of-place sons.

I remember attending a meeting as a young preacher boy. I can't remember who was preaching—or even much of what he talked about—but one thing he said has stuck with me for almost fifty years. He was talking about the Holy Trinity's involvement in seeking out those who are lost. These are not his exact words, but here is what I heard in my spirit: "God thought it, the Holy Spirit sought it, and Jesus bought it." God is one God, but three coeternal and consubstantial persons: the Father, the Son (Jesus Christ), and the Holy Spirit. The three persons are distinct, yet they are one substance, essence, or nature.

If I had the assignment of reducing this parable down to three simple statements, this would be my choice: God thought it, the Holy Spirit sought it, and the Son bought it. This is the Father's heart.

The heart of God toward humans is revealed in this story. When you keep this in mind as you read the parable, you will discover what God thinks about you, how God sees you, and how God feels about you. These are the three primary questions humanity has wrestled with since the fall of humanity in Genesis 3. Most people are not sure how God feels about them, how he sees them, and how he feels about them. It makes it harder for a prodigal to come home if they're not sure the Father will welcome them.

Without knowing his father would let him stay if he came home, the young runaway son got to his feet, set his face and heart toward home, and took his first step in the right direction. A journey of any length begins with the first step.

## The Homecoming

> And while he was still a long way off, his father saw
> him coming. Filled with love and compassion, he
> ran to his son, embraced him, and kissed him. His
> son said to him, "Father, I have sinned against both
> heaven and you, and I am no longer worthy to be
> called your son." (Luke 15:20–21 NLTV)

How was it possible for the father to see his young son while he
was still a long way off if he had not been looking for him? He is
the one with the searching heart. I can see him standing out by the
road every day, looking, and thinking, *Is this the day my son will
come home?* Every movement along the roadway must have gotten
his attention and aroused his hope. Then it happened! "That's him;
that's my son coming. I would recognize that walk anywhere."

The father did not hesitate. He ran to his son with a heart full
of love and compassion. When the father got to his son, he grabbed
him and started kissing him rapidly and repeatedly, and the son was
not able to give his entire homecoming speech:

> I am no longer worthy to be called your son. Make
> me one of your hired servants. (Luke 15:19 NKJV)

The boy must have been confused. *When will the lecture come?*
*"I knew the day would get here when you would come home with your
tail tucked between your legs." The "I told you" sermon has got to be
delivered soon. "I knew you didn't have what it took to make it out
there on your own."* The out-of-place son wasn't met with a sermon
or a lecture. Instead, he was inundated with love and compassion.
He was the recipient of an abundance of grace, something he did
not deserve. The returning prodigal found grace in his father's home
because grace was in his father's heart.

I'm sure the religious spirits in the crowd began to squirm even more when Jesus shared this part of the story. Grace always rattles a religious spirit. They could have handled it a whole lot better if the prodigal had received justice for his chosen lifestyle. These religious snakes would have choked on their own venom if the father had extended mercy to his son. But grace? That's taking it way too far.

Why does grace easily offend? We certainly want grace shown to us when we mess up, but we are reluctant to give it to others. Is it possible to share our father's home but not our father's heart? Yes. We will deal with this in chapter 6 when we take a close look at the oldest son who stayed home. He never ran away from home, but he had walked away mentally and emotionally. He shared his father's home, but he did not share his father's heart.

## Grace offends

Far too many believers are offended by pure, unadulterated grace— unless they are in need of it. This is what God's grace is. Since God is thrice holy, everything about him is pure and unadulterated (Isaiah 6:3 NKJV). When he extends his grace to us, it is unmixed. God's grace is pure.

Here is a short made-up story that may help shine a light on how incredible God's grace is. An employee at a local bank was caught embezzling money. A special meeting was called by the board of directors to discuss their plan of action. The chairman of the board presented three options for the directors to consider.

The first option was justice. They could report the guilty individual to the legal authorities and let the justice system handle it. In due process, punishment would be metered out. Justice is getting what you deserve.

The second option was mercy. They could immediately terminate the guilty party. There would be no severance pay or any other benefits given. The board would agree not to notify the authorities, their family members, or anyone else. The issue would be kept secret among the board members. Anyone in that situation would deeply appreciate receiving mercy. Mercy is not getting what you deserve.

The third option was grace. They could promote this individual to vice president. The promotion would more than triple their pay—and more vacation time would be given. They would also be given a company credit card with no credit limit. A clothing allowance would be given, which would also include their family members. A college fund would be set up by the bank to pay for the children's education. This new position would entitle them to the use of a company car. The vehicle could be for personal use, and all fuel costs would be taken care of by the bank. Grace is getting what you don't deserve.

How do you feel when you read the grace option? What are your thoughts? Most would have to admit they feel a little miffed—if not outraged. "This is not fair!" I know. This is why it's called grace. Now you know how the religious folks in the crowd must have felt when they heard Jesus explain how the father received his son, the prodigal. Grace is getting what you do not deserve

The biggest misconception about grace is that it will give a person a license to sin. Have you noticed that people don't need a license to sin? Most people seem to be faring well in the sin area. Grace does not give us a license to sin; grace gives us the freedom and liberty of not wanting to sin because grace changes our *want to.* When a person begins to understand they are recipients of God's pure grace, they won't be sinless—but they will sin less. Grace doesn't free us to sin; grace frees us from sin.

The prodigal son was more than willing to be treated like a slave. The servants in his father's house had better lives than he was living in the faraway country. Instead, he found himself in the embrace of his loving father. His father received and treated him like who he was—a son. His bad behavior did not change his genetics as the father's son.

## True Repentance: Change of Mind, Change in Direction

With his father smothering him with hugs and kisses, the son tried to deliver his pigpen speech:

> Father, I have sinned against heaven and in your sight, and am no longer worthy to be called your son. (Luke 15:21 NKJV)

Don't let what he did not say slip by you: "Make me like one of your servants." These words never came out of his mouth (Luke 15:19 NKJV). Why? Repentance was enough. These words could not be spoken because the love and affection of the father for his son washed them away. He was a son by birth, and he would be no less because of his behavior.

The word repentance (metanoia) means a change of mind that leads to a compete change in direction. It's a 180-degree turn toward God. This young man's repentance produced a confession:

> I have sinned against heaven and in your sight. (Luke 15:21 NKJV)

Confession (*homologeo*) means to say the same thing that God says. His mouth was now in alignment with his mind. This young man's repentance took place in the pen with the pigs. His change of mind turned him in the right direction. Standing before his father, he made his repentant heart known: "I have sinned against both heaven and you." His confession was saying the same thing as his repentant mind.

Most people think repentance is all about what we say. This is why so many people continue to struggle with sin issues. They will tell you that they have repented time and time again to no avail. For some reason, they can't find victory over a specific sin. Repentance has nothing to do with the mouth and what we say. It is about changing our minds about sin and going in the opposite direction.

When we think about sin the way God thinks about sin, we will have a hard time choosing to sin or enjoying sin.

Let's say that we have decided to eat dinner at a certain Italian restaurant. On our way to the restaurant, we come to agreement that Mexican food sounds good, change our minds, and go in the opposite direction to eat Mexican food instead of Italian. The next day, we are talking to some friends about dinner the night before. We could say, "Last night, we were headed to eat Italian food, but on the way to the restaurant, we *repented,* went in the opposite direction, and ate Mexican food. We repented. We changed our minds. We went in another direction."

This is what happened to the prodigal when he was in the pigsty. He came to his senses. He snapped and realized where he was and how he got there. He had a change of mind. His decision was to leave the pigs, a place he did not belong, and go to where he *did* belong: with his father.

## The Father's Heart Revealed

If you want to know what the Father thinks about you, how he sees you, and how he feels about you, take a slow walk through this story—and pay attention to how the father talks to and interacts with his two sons. This is what Jesus wants us to know about our heavenly Father. He is the one who never changes (Malachi 3:6 NKJV). If he loves us when we are behaving right, he will love us when we behave wrong because he never changes. When we discover this about our heavenly Father's nature, it will affect the way we behave and the choices we make in a good way.

God is unchanging in his purity and in his perfection. God is immutable in his perfection and in his promises. God can never get better, and he can never get worse.

We can imagine how bad this young man must have smelled when his father engaged him with hugs and kisses on the road as he approached home. The smell of pigs and the scent of sin-soiled clothes must have been overpowering. It didn't impede the father from showing the affection he had for his son. Nothing was said about how bad the prodigal needed a bath and a change of clothes. It didn't slow the father down one bit. He was too excited to have his son home where he belonged to be offended by his appearance and smell:

> And above all things have fervent love for one another, *for love will cover a multitude of sins.* (1 Peter 4:8 NKJV; emphasis added)

We see love covering in this story.

What does it mean when we say the heart of God? If the heart of God is revealed in this story, what is being revealed? The heart is an expression of the nature of something, the very core or essence of something. In having a deep discussion about a particular subject, we could say, "Let's cut to the chase, deal with the heart of the matter, and dig down to the core."

The heart of God is his nature. It is the very core of his being, his essence. Contrary to what many believe, God is not a cosmic cop patrolling stealthily in search of religious violators. He finds no sadistic pleasure in administering corporal punishment to those who kick against the goads.

One of the purposes for telling this story about the father and his two sons is for us to know that our heavenly Father has a heart full of compassion. This is an alien concept to the Pharisees and scribes. This was very offensive for them to hear. They could only relate to God based on the rules and regulations they were required to keep. Under their system, this young man would have been stoned in the city streets for his behavior. You can almost hear their teeth grinding and an occasional snort as Jesus talked about the compassion this father smothered the prodigal son with. Compassion is a part of God's nature. It's one of the attributes that make him who he is:

> But You, O Lord, are a God full of compassion, and gracious, Longsuffering and abundant in mercy and truth. (Psalm 86:15 NKJV)

This story also reveals that our heavenly Father has a heart full of unconditional love. The prodigal son violated every condition that is required for being a good son. He demanded his part of the estate while his father was still alive. In essence, he was saying, "I wish you were dead." How cold. How callous. He never considered the feelings of his father. He made life about himself and what he wanted.

When he came to the end of himself, alone and destitute, he made the decision to return to his father. Instead of being placed on probation, lectured, or preached to, the son was received with unconditional love—with no strings attached. Even though he deserved to be turned away and rejected, the father loved him unconditionally.

The heart of God is full of compassion, unconditional love, and grace. The prodigal found grace in his father's house because grace was in his father's heart. Grace is unlike justice, which is getting what you deserve. Grace is different than mercy, which is not getting what you deserve. Grace is getting what you don't deserve.

At this point in the story, I can see the hair on the back of the necks of the Pharisees and scribes standing at attention. They are seething with anger! This is not the God they know. Here's the sad commentary. This is not the God that most believers know either. If it were, we would not have as many runaways as we do. More would be running to the Father and not away from him. It is so much easier to run to someone who is full of compassion, running over with unconditional love, and full of grace:

> And the Spirit and the bride say, "Come!" And let him who hears say, "Come!" And let him who thirsts come. Whoever desires, let him take the water of life freely. (Revelation 22:17 NKJV)

## This Story Is Our Story

Hopefully, by now, you know that the main characters in this story are not the two sons. It is the father and how he responds to the people the two sons represent. This story is actually filled with characters like you and me. At any moment in life, we can find ourselves wearing the sandals of the oldest son or the sandals of the youngest son. All it takes is a new day. The flashing sign in the local sandal shop reads: "Prodigal Shoes: One Size Fits All.

The father's youngest son could not live like a son because he thought like a slave. A slave mentality will keep you from knowing your true identity. Too many Christians are not living up to their identities as children of God because they have no clue who they are. The father's oldest son could not think like a son because he lived like a slave. It's hard to be who you don't know you are. Neither son was living up to their identity. They couldn't enjoy what they had because they didn't know who they were.

Does this sound familiar? It should. These two sons represent the majority of believers. It is one thing to know you are a child of God, but it is another to think and live like a child of God. Most Christians live their entire lives and never make the discovery of who they are in Christ. They don't know their true identity. If you think like a slave, you will live like a slave. If you live like a slave, you will think like a slave.

What God thinks about you is revealed through the heart of this father in the way he loves his sons. Even with their slave mentality, he loves them for who they are—and not by how they behave. How he sees you and how he feels about you are not based on what you do; they are based on what he has done.

This may be a good time to hear what the great philosopher Dennis the Menace had to say about goodness. Many years ago, there was a cartoon of Dennis and his sidekick, Joey, walking away from his neighbors, the Wilsons. Both boys had their hands full of cookies.

Joey looks at Dennis and said, "I wonder what we did to deserve this."

Dennis responded, "Look, Joey. Mrs. Wilson did not give us cookies because we are good. We got cookies because Mrs. Wilson is good."

The father did not scold or lecture his son for his decision to leave home and ending up making a mess out of his life. He did not belittle him for the bad choices he made or put him on probation. And it was not because his son was good. It was because the father is good. All the father said was, "Let's get the party started."

CHAPTER  FIVE

# THE CELEBRATION

---

## The Robe, the Ring, the Sandals, and the Barbecue

Have you noticed how much partying is going on in this story that Jesus is telling the up-and-outs (Pharisees and scribes) as well as the down-and-outs (tax collectors and sinners)? When the man finds his lost sheep, he calls his neighbors and friends together and says, "Rejoice with me, for I have found my sheep which was lost" (Luke 15:6 NKJV). He is ready to celebrate because he found the sheep that was out of place. Jesus ends this part of the story with these words:

> I say to you that likewise there will be more joy in heaven over one sinner who repents than over ninety-nine just persons who need no repentance. (Luke 15:7 NKJV)

This tells us that Jesus is not talking about four-footed animals.

As soon as he finishes his sheep story, Jesus tells them about the woman who searched for and found the piece of silver that was lost. The first thing she did when she found it was call her friends and neighbors over for a celebration:

> Rejoice with me, for I have found the piece which I
> lost. (Luke 15:9 NKJV)

Jesus immediately tells us what this lost piece of silver represents:

> Likewise, I say to you, there is joy in the presence
> of the angels of God over one sinner who repents.
> (Luke 15:10 NKJV)

Once again, Jesus is not talking about a silver coin. It is something more important than that.

Now we have a father throwing a huge party to celebrate his youngest son's return home. Just like the sheep and the silver, the son had been lost but was found:

> [For] this my son was dead and is alive again; he
> was lost and is found. And they began to be merry.
> (Luke 15:24 NKJV)

> It was right that we should make merry and be glad,
> for your brother was dead and is alive again and was
> lost and is found. (Luke 15:32 NKJV)

Jesus wanted those who were listening to him to know how heaven responds when a lost soul—a soul that is out of place—is put back where it belongs. Heaven celebrates.

In the next chapter, Jesus tells another story. This time, it is about a lost soul (Luke 16:19–31 NKJV). This story does not end with a party. There is no celebration in heaven over a soul that has been lost for eternity. God the Father and his angels do not celebrate a soul that is forever out of place.

## The Celebration Preparation

Now that the youngest son was back where he belonged, it was time to celebrate. The father began to give party instructions to his servants. Nothing was to be held back on the festivities. The father went all out. Whole hog! After all, it was not a sheep or a silver coin that had been found. It was his son. The band was assembling, the neighbors were coming, gifts were being gathered, and the cook fire was ignited. The fatted calf was nervous. It was time to celebrate!

If we get totally absorbed with the party preparations, we might miss something that is significant. The Pharisees and scribes were fuming. The grinding of their teeth could be heard a block away:

> Now the Pharisees, who are lovers of money, *also heard all these things*, and they *derided* him. (Luke 16:14 NKJV; emphasis added)

You can probably picture their upper lips curled in disdain. They had an aristocratic religious disdain for this young man they did not know. "He doesn't deserve a party. What he needs is to be taken to the middle of the street and be stoned to death by all the family members and friends for his behavior. Instead they are celebrating him."

## Celebration Gifts: The Best Robe

The father told his servants to put the best robe on his son. There are two things that are worth noting. It wasn't just a robe the father told his servants to put on his son. It was the best robe. Nothing but the best for his son. The robe was to be placed on him right away—and not after he bathed and cleaned up. Interesting.

Could Jesus have had the words of the prophet Isaiah in mind?

> I will greatly rejoice in the Lord, My soul shall be joyful in my God; For *He has clothed me with the garments of salvation, He has covered me with the robe of righteousness.* (Isaiah 61:10 NKJV; emphasis added)

The son—who did nothing to deserve it—was wearing the father's best robe. It covered his filth-and-sin-soiled garments. It was a garment of salvation, a robe of righteousness. The word righteousness means to be upright, in right standing. He was out of place, but now he was back where he belonged: in right standing with his father.

Wow! This young man was fresh from the pigpen. The filth from the pigsty was still oozing between his toes. He reeked from the stench of the world, but he was standing before his father clothed in the best robe, a robe of right standing. He was where he belonged. He was back in place. What a father! The only thing the father could give was the *best robe.*

We are able to see the differences between justice, mercy, and grace that we talked about earlier. Grace is getting what you don't deserve. This was what the father was doing. He was not giving the youngest son what he deserved. He was giving him what he did not deserve—grace—because the father's heart was full of grace to the repentant.

It is significant that the best robe was the first gift the father gave his son. It symbolized that the son had been accepted by the father. The robe represented the robe of righteousness that was provided through the shed blood of Jesus Christ. The robe symbolized that we are accepted and declared not guilty before the Lord. Once again, what a father!

Untold numbers of people have a desire to come to the father, but they believe the lie that they must clean up their act first. If you have to clean up your act before you come to the Father, how much do you have to clean up: 50 percent, 75 percent, or 90 percent? How much?

Charlotte Elliott wrote a hymn about how to find salvation through Christ. It is a simple message of sin, forgiveness, and salvation to all who turn from sin and trust in Christ. "Just as I am" was written in 1835. There is no telling how many times it was sung for the invitation at a Billy Graham crusade:

Just as I am, without one plea
But that Thy blood was shed for me
And that Thou bid'st me come to Thee
O Lamb of God, I come! I come
Just as I am, though tossed about
With many a conflict, many a doubt
Fighting and fears within without
O Lamb of God, I come, I come
Just as I am, and waiting not
to rid my soul of one dark blot
to thee whose blood can cleanse each spot
O Lamb of God, I come, I come
Just as I am, poor, wretched, blind
Sight, riches, healing of the mind
Yea, all I need, in Thee to find
O Lamb of God, I come, I come!
Just as I am, Thou wilt receive
Wilt welcome, pardon, cleanse, relieve
Because Thy promise I believe
O Lamb of God, I come, I come
Because Thy promise I believe
O Lamb of God, I come, I come

The prodigal son came to his father just the way he was: marred by sin, soiled, and stained. His father received him just the way he was. To show that he was fully accepted, the father covered him with the best robe. It was a robe of right standing.

Coming home was proving to be the best decision the young

man had made in a long time. During his lonely walk home, he had to fight through the lies that were going through his head about being rejected by his father. The enemy wants all prodigals to think that once you have taken *steps of rebellion*, you might as well keep running because you will be forever rejected by the Father. Many are on the lam today because they have believed this lie.

There is no shortage of "best robes" in the Father's house.


## Celebration Gift: The Ring

The next command the father gave his servants was this: "Put a ring on my son's hand" (Luke 15:22 NKJV). The boy gets a ring? Since he's wearing the best robe, it's time for some serious bling. Are you kidding me? Maybe Jesus is taking this story about grace too far. Once again, you can hear the deep groans coming from the Pharisees and scribes. Without bathing, he gets the best robe—and now he's being given a ring? Always remember, whatever God is, he is completely. Since he is good, he is completely good. (Maybe it would be a good idea to go back and reread the definition of grace in chapter 4.)

The robe was a sign that the father had welcomed his son back to where he belonged. By giving him a ring, the father was making another statement. The prodigal was welcomed back—and he had been restored to a place of responsibility and authority. The ring represents identity. It's the same thing as the family credit card. In business transactions, the signet ring would be used to make its print in wax to mark a document as having been written by the one owning the signet ring.

Maybe the father had a short memory. Had he forgotten that his son wasted his livelihood on wild living? He had already demonstrated he couldn't be trusted with material possessions. And now the father gives him the key to the family treasury? Here's some great news. The prodigal may have wasted his livelihood, but he did not lose his inheritance. The gift of a ring symbolizes a transfer of inheritance.

The ring is a sign of covenant. Your covenant with God the Father cannot be breached or broken by any external force. He is yours, and you are His. Just like a ring is a complete circle, showing no sign of beginning or ending, God's love for you is eternal. That means he loves you with a love that has no beginning and no end. God's love for you is based on who he is and not by what you have or have not done.

When we made our decision to accept Christ's offer for eternal life, we were given a new identity. We became new creations. No longer are we children of flesh and blood, bearing human genetics. We are now children of God, through the gift of the Holy Spirit, which gives us our divine genetics:

> But as many as received Him, to them He gave the right to become children of God, to those who believe in Him. (John 1:12 NKJV)

> The Spirit Himself bears witness with our spirit that we are children of God. (Romans 8:16 NKJV)

Now that we have been made righteous, it's time to start living like we are in covenant with God the Father.

## Celebration Gift: Sandals

The prodigal son went home barefooted. You could say that he literally had nothing to stand on. Pun intended. When he left home, he was shod with good sandals. I wonder what happened to them. Had he lost them or hocked them in a pawnshop? We really don't know. To come home without shoes reveals just how destitute this young man had become. In biblical times, only servants and slaves went barefoot.

Maybe the answer to the missing sandals is tucked away in the story:

> Then he [the prodigal] went and *joined himself* to a
> citizen of that country, and he sent him into his fields
> to feed swine. (Luke 15:15 NKJV; emphasis added)

To join himself means to be taken into slavery. Once you became a slave, your sandals were taken away to prevent you from running away. This young man was living like a slave because he was thinking like a slave. This is how a child of God lives when they live life out of place.

In that time and culture, shoes differentiated a son from a slave. An untold number of sons and daughters today are living like slaves because they have surrendered their identities. They have voluntarily relinquished their sandals to the masters of this world. When you give up your shoes as a child of God, you cannot enjoy your birthright privileges. Most believers are not even aware of their birthright privileges.

The father ordered his servants to put sandals on his son's feet. This was the third time the father demonstrated that the prodigal was not a servant or slave; he was a son with all the entitlements. The father wanted his son to know that he was not a servant in his home. It was also a signal to everyone in the house, including the oldest son. Now that he was wearing the shoes of a son, he needed to stop living and thinking like a slave.

The Pharisees and scribes had to be apoplectic by then. Jesus had taken the story about grace over the top. The message of grace will always offend a religious spirit. How could this father be so generous to this young man after all he had done? He didn't deserve what the father was giving him. If the father had taken the prodigal to the streets to have him stoned, the Pharisees and scribes would have been more than happy to participate. They would have gotten some warped pleasure in doing so.

## The Celebration Gift: The Fatted Calf

> [And] bring the fatted calf here and kill it, and let
> us eat and be merry; for this my son was dead and
> is alive again; he was lost and is found. And they
> began to be merry. (Luke 15:23–24 NKJV)

These are the instructions the father gave his servants. I wonder who hated to see the youngest son come home the most: the eldest son or the calf. It may have been a toss-up. There's one thing we do know for certain: the fatted calf made the biggest contribution to the celebration.

The party was about to pick up steam. The aroma of the barbecue was beginning to fill the air. The sound of music could be heard from a distance. The volume of chatter coming from the guests was getting louder. The servants were busy catering to the partygoers. The party was definitely gaining momentum.

Can you imagine the emotions that were flooding through the youngest son's soul? Just a few hours earlier, he had been walking toward home with his head filled with doubts. Would he be received by his father or be turned away—or even stoned. He was now the honored guest of a huge celebration.

Try to picture this party scene in your mind. The father was standing close to the barbecue pit where the fatted calf was making its contribution to the celebration. Standing next to the father was his youngest son with the father's best robe, a sparkling ring on his finger, and new leather sandals on his feet. I wonder what was going through his mind. What gift do you think had him the most captivated? Was it the best robe that covered his sin-soiled body? Maybe it was the family credit card he had on his finger. Could it be the beautiful shoes that supported his bruised and aching feet or the fatted calf that was emitting an incredible aroma?

I doubt very seriously if any of these gifts, incredible as they may be, captured his attention. I'm convinced he couldn't take his eyes off of his father. His gaze was locked in on the one who had given him the gifts. His entire focus was on his father—the one who had restored him back to where he belonged.

The father had the well-fed calf killed to show that this celebration was out of the ordinary. It was not just a neighborhood block party. It was a special occasion, and the only way to really celebrate it was to kill the fatted calf. Not just any calf would do. It had to be the one that had been well-fed for special occasions. No occasion in the eyes of heaven is more important than a sinner, someone who is out of place, coming to their senses and returning to where they belong: with the Father in his house.

## You Can Get Glad in the Same Britches You Get Mad In

It is easy to get so involved with this story that we lose sight of why Jesus told it. When we read it or hear it taught, we get excited. It encourages our hearts. This was not true for many who were in the crowd that day. Let's reshape the story within its context.

Jesus was hanging out with the sinners. As a matter of fact, he had the audacity to eat with them. Eating with sinners went beyond the pale for these self-righteous synagogue leaders. If you have any religious savvy at all, you know that you don't fellowship with sinners, especially tax collectors. The Pharisees and scribes could not handle this, and they let their voices be heard:

> The Pharisees and scribes complained, saying, "This Man [Jesus] receives sinners and eats with them." (Luke 15:2 NKJV)

When Jesus heard these words, "He spoke this parable to them" (Luke 15:3 NKJV). Even though "the sinners" heard Jesus tell this story, the main audience was the religious snobs. They were anything but blessed and encouraged by it.

At this juncture, the religious extremists started expressing their contempt for Jesus. They mocked and ridiculed him (Luke 16:14 NKJV). Their God would never associate with sinners, those who are out of place. How dare Jesus to say he would? They have no clue they were seeing and hearing God the Father in human form in the person of Jesus Christ:

> For the Son of Man has come to seek and to save
> that which was lost. (Luke 19:10 NKJV)

Jesus was telling them that God the Father loves the one sheep that is lost. He is searching for the one lost piece of silver. The Father is looking for all the lost sons and daughters to come home where they belong. And when they do come home, there will be huge celebration in heaven. They will be embraced in the arms of grace.

This parable answers these three questions: What does God think about you? How does God see you? How does God feel about you? If you think these religious fanatics were mad then, wait until the next chapter when Jesus deals with the walkaway prodigal: the elder son.

CHAPTER  SIX

# THE WALKAWAY PRODIGAL

—————

### He Shared His Father's Home but Not His Father's Heart

We are about to be introduced to the father's oldest son. This young man was where good sons were supposed to be. He was working in the field—and he was working hard. After a long day in the field, he was making his way back to the house. He was probably thinking about all that he'd been able to accomplish that day and what the next day would look like. It was time to wash up for the evening meal. As he was approaching the house, he could hear the celebration taking place. The closer he got, the louder the music and dancing became.

A couple of things jump out at me in this part of the story. I can understand that he could hear the music, but when you can hear dancing, you have a party going on! It was certainly not your average get-together.

The second thing that grabs my attention is that not one servant felt it was necessary to go to the field and tell him about his brother's return or the celebration the father was throwing for the occasion. Could it be the servants knew him pretty well? Since they knew how he would react, no one felt compelled to give him the good news about his brother coming home. He would find out soon enough.

The elder brother asked one of the servants what was going on.

> *Your brother* has come, and because he has received him safe and sound, your father has killed *the fatted calf.* (Luke 15:27 NKJV; emphasis added)

The servants answer reminded the eldest brother of something he wanted to forget: his family tie with his younger brother. When he heard the news about the fatted calf being killed, he knew how serious his father was about celebrating the return of his brother. By the way, the oldest son still had his sandals on. Just because you are wearing the sandals of a son, you can still think and live like a slave. It's possible to stand in your identity and not live out your birthright.

> But he was angry and would not go in. (Luke 15:28 NKJV)

Why would the oldest son be so angry when his father was so happy about his youngest son coming home? He was not the only who was mad. Don't forget about the Pharisees and the scribes. They were fired up too because they knew that Jesus was talking about them. They were wearing the same sandals the elder brother is wearing.

The elder brother was mad because he didn't think his younger brother was getting what he deserved. As a matter of fact, he was getting what he didn't deserve. He should have been stoned for what he did—or at least be scolded and sent away. Place him on probation, but for crying out loud, don't throw a party in his honor. Grace is very upsetting to those who wear elder brother sandals.

The celebration offended the ears of the elder brother, and he refused to enter the house:

Therefore his father came out and pleaded with him. (Luke 15:28 NKJV)

It was the father who initiated the contact with the oldest son, which was the same reaction the father had when he saw his youngest son coming down the road. He didn't wait until he got to the house. He ran to him. The father went outside and pleaded with his eldest son to go in and join the celebration. The father loved his oldest son the same way he loved his youngest son. His heart was toward both of them. He was a good father.

## The Walkaway Son's Speech

The oldest son delivered a speech to his father that he had probably been working on for a long time. The youngest son put his speech together while he was in the pen with the pigs. The eldest son probably had written his speech over time while doing his chores and steaming over his youngest brother leaving him with all the chores. He had been working like one of the slaves:

> So he answered and said to his father, "Lo, these many years I have been *serving* you; I never transgressed your commandment at any time; and yet you never gave me a young goat, that I might make merry with my friends." (Luke 15:29 NKJV; emphasis added)

The word *serving* can be translated as *slaving*. The eldest son was venting his true feelings. The words coming out of his mouth had probably been secretly kept in his heart for some time:

> Out of the abundance of the heart, the mouth speaks. (Luke 6:45 NKJV)

The elder brother's speech may have sounded something like this: "Dad, for years, I have been slaving for you. I have never refused to do anything you have told me to do. Not one time have you given me a goat so I could have a barbecue with my friends. When this son of yours comes home—after squandering your money on prostitutes and wild living—you celebrate by killing the fatted calf? It's just not fair." It seems like he is trying to build himself up by tearing his brother down.

The older son's speech reveals his heart. Even though he is a son, he has been living like a servant because he thinks like a slave:

> All these years I have *slaved* for you. (Luke 15:29 NLT; emphasis added)

He had a slave's mentality. I seriously doubt he had any friends either.

The older son was the only one in the father's house who could not, or would not, rejoice over what has happened. His brother had a change of heart and had come home to where he belonged. He was acting just like the Pharisees who considered themselves righteous. They never missed a synagogue service. They might have had big scowls on their faces when they went, but you could count on them being in their special pews. Whatever you did, you didn't make the mistake of sitting in one of their seats. You would get one of *those* looks. To the Pharisees, their external actions were more important than their internal attitudes.

It sounds like the youngest son was not the only one wallowing in the pigpen. While his pigpen experience happened in a faraway country, the elder brother was wallowing in the pigpen of resentment, jealousy, and unforgiveness. He could not rejoice over his brother's change of heart because he did not share his father's heart. There's only one way out of the pigpen. We must be willing to admit that we have sinned and fallen short of the glory of the Father. The prodigal's confession came while he was in the pigsty:

> Father, I have sinned against heaven and in your sight. (Luke 15:21 NKJV)

This was his first step from bondage to freedom. The elder brother was facing the same option, but he chose not to take it.

The elder brother also had a short memory. He told his father that he had slaved for him for years and had never refused to do anything he asked him to do (Luke 15:29 NKJV). Maybe he had forgotten the times he disobeyed his father's instructions. Is it humanly possible to go through the maturation process from boyhood to manhood without ever disobeying? It is also possible to do the right thing with the wrong attitude.

The anger he had for the way his father was treating his youngest brother was so strong that he refused to acknowledge him as his brother: "This son of yours" (Luke 15:30 NKJV). Can't you hear the elder brother saying, "Dad, have you forgotten that your youngest son has wasted your livelihood on riotous living? And you killed the fatted calf for him? You have got to be kidding me!" I can hear the Pharisees and scribes saying, "Amen, brother, preach it."

The older brother had not run away from home like his younger brother had, but he had walked away a long time ago in his mind. He shared his father's home, but he did not share his father's heart. He was so focused on what he thought he didn't have that he couldn't see what he did have. He was a walkaway prodigal.

Our church buildings are filled with walkway sons and daughters. Oh, they fill their chairs on Sundays, and they continue doing their chores, ushering, greeting, singing. But mentally and emotionally, they left a long time ago. Their bodies are still in the house, but their hearts have walked away. If you don't believe this, then open your ears and listen to what they say the next time a prodigal comes home. They will not join in the celebration.

When a prodigal who has truly repented comes to the Father, they are received with the sweet arms of grace. A prodigal is received by an elder brother with the strong arm of the law. More prodigals would be returning to where they belong if they did not have to deal with the elder brothers. Since the elder brothers are impossible to please, they assume the Father is as well.

## The Father's Heart toward His Oldest Son

The father responded to his hard-hearted eldest son with the same extravagant grace he had given his youngest son when he came home. He addressed him as son:

> And he said to him, "*Son*, you are always with me, and all that I have is yours." (Luke 15:31 NKJV; emphasis added)

Even though the elder brother refused to acknowledge that the father's youngest son was his brother, the father addressed him as his son. The elder brother was acting like a servant and talking like a slave, but the father treated him like a son.

The father wanted his oldest son to know that no matter how he acted—regardless of what he said—he still saw him as his son. *Son* is a term of intimacy. The father reminded him, "You are always with me" (Luke 15:31 NKJV). It doesn't matter if we are in the pigpen in some faraway country or in a pigsty in our own minds, the Father's heart is always toward us. He will never leave us or forsake us (Hebrews 13:5 NKJV). He is a good Father, and whatever he is, he is completely. Since he is good, he is completely good.

The father also reminded his elder son of what he had: "All that I have are yours" (Luke 15:31 NKJV). If our focus is lasered in on what we think we don't have, it will blind us to what we do have. Had the elder son forgotten what his father did when the youngest son demanded his livelihood so he could move out and be his own boss?

And the younger son said to his father, "Father, give me the portion of goods that falls to me." *So he divided to them his livelihood.* (Luke 15:12 NKJV; emphasis added)

Oh, look at that. The father divided his livelihood between both sons. The elder son got his share too. Isn't it amazing how soon we forget our blessings?

The father wanted his eldest son to know why it was a time for celebrating. And in doing so, he reminded the elder son of his family ties:

This is a great day, son. *Your brother* was dead and has come back to life! He was lost but now he is found. You may not want to admit it but he is your brother. Celebrating his return is the right thing to do. (Luke 15:32 NLT)

## There Is No Shortage of Elder Brothers in the Family of Faith

Why are elder brothers so hard to please? Why do they get so angry when prodigals repent and come home? It's because they believe something that is not true. The Pharisees and scribes are aghast at this story Jesus was telling. This story about lost sheep, silver, and sons was about them—and they knew it.

In 2002, George Barna Research Group polled Christians nationwide to find out why *legalism* was so widespread. They were interested in why believers were so focused on living life by obeying rules and the law rather than having a relationship with God through Jesus Christ by the power of the Holy Spirit. We are talking about the American church.

Here's what one out of every six surveyed believe the Christian life is all about. One out of every six believed the Christian life is trying to do what God commands: 57 percent strongly agreed with this, and 25 percent agreed somewhat. Think about this: 82 percent of the Christians polled believed that the Christian life is trying to do what God commands.

There is one huge problem with the results of this survey. It is not true. This is not what Christianity is about. This is performance-based religion. This is what the elder son believed as well as the Pharisees and scribes. Christianity is not about what we can do for Christ; it is what he's done for us. The Word of God clearly states that we come to God the Father by grace and not by works (Ephesians 2:8–9 NKJV).

What good works had the prodigal son done that forced the father to take him back? Can you name one? When he came to his father, the only thing he had was a sin-stained life. All he had was a life he had messed up. That's it. He came just the way he was. He found out that the father was willing to clean up what he had messed up.

A group of people was questioning Jesus one day about good works:

> Then they said to Him, "What shall we do that we may work the works of God?" Jesus answered and said to them, "This is the work of God, that you believe in Him whom He sent." (John 6:28–20 NKJV)

The work that is required for us to be in right standing with the Father is to believe.

The elder brother is to be commended for his hard work, but it was not his work that made him a son. He was born a son. He had nothing to do or say about that. It wasn't his behavior that determined his sonship; it was his birth. Working hard was not his issue. His Achilles' heel was his attitude.

The elder brother reminds me of the little boy who was standing up in the back seat of the car as his father drove him to school. When the father saw him in the rearview mirror, he told him to sit down. The boy flopped down in disgust.

It wasn't long before the father noticed his son was standing up. Again, he told him to sit down. This happened a few more times before they got to school. Finally, the father said, "If I catch you standing up again, I'm going to stop the car and give you a spanking."

The little boy slammed himself down in the car seat, crossed his arms, stuck out his bottom lip, and said, "I may be sitting down, but I'm standing up on the inside."

This is how I see the elder brother. He might be sitting down, but he's standing up on the inside. His actions and his attitude did not congeal. He did the right thing, but he did it with the wrong attitude.

At that point, the Pharisees and scribes were boiling over with hatred for Jesus. He had eviscerated them with his story. They knew he was talking about them and how they felt and treated the sinners of this world. Their pharisaical spirit had been exposed for all to see.

## Similarities between the Two Sons

The elder son and the younger son were alike in many respects, but at the same time, they were very different. Keep in mind that the Pharisees and scribes understand what Jesus was saying. They had something in common with both sons. The youngest son was rebellious and estranged from his father while he lived away from his father's home. The elder son was rebellious and estranged from his father even though he lived in his father's home. One left physically, and one left emotionally—but both had left. It's possible to be present and absent at the same time.

The difference between the two was in their willingness to

acknowledge their rebellion. The youngest son came to his senses while living with the pigs. He had a come-to-the-father moment. He got to his feet, returned to his father, and confessed his sin. The elder's son's rebellion remained in his heart. His hypocrisy was hidden and had hardened. He remained in the house with his father even though he had lost respect for his father. He denied he had any relationship with his younger brother. He also denied any relationship with his father: "This son of yours" (Luke 15:30 NKJV). He never said, "My father."

The family of faith has many who live the same way as the elder brother. They are rule-following people. They are task-oriented folks. They are hard workers. If they are faithful enough, they will earn their birthright privileges. In their heart of hearts, they know that salvation is not earned by their good deeds. Even though they believe in the fundamentals of the faith, they are convinced that, somehow, they have to earn their place of acceptance. They think that working *harder* enhances their chances.

Working hard did not make the elder brother more of a son. Not working hard did not make the younger brother less of a son. Their sonship was determined by their birth. They became a part of the family by birth—not by their behaviors. Neither was living up to their identity as sons.

## Intimacy and Inheritance

> And he [the father] said to him, "Son, you are always with me, and all that I have is yours." (Luke 15:31 NKJV)

The father reminded his eldest son about the family intimacy they shared as father and son. The oldest son had access to everything the father had because he was family. The father did not withhold anything from the elder brother. All that the father had was his.

When we see people getting what they don't deserve, we have a tendency to become jealous. Jealousy can lead to resentment and bitterness, which cause us to lose sight of what we've been blessed with. We are unable to see what we have because we are so consumed with what others are getting.

It was the father who went outside to talk to his eldest son because he had refused to go inside and join the celebration. The father's heart was toward his oldest son in the same measure as it was toward the prodigal. He wanted him to be a part of the celebration. If the roles were reversed, the celebration would have been for him. The father did everything he could to reason with his oldest son. The elder brother's response was one complaint after another.

I saw an interesting sign: "As you waste your breath complaining about life, someone out there is breathing their last. Appreciate what you have." It is hard to appreciate what we have when we spend the majority of our time in the complaint department.

## Back to the Audience of This Story

The hero in this story for the Pharisees and scribes has to be the walkaway son. He was a hard worker and had no tolerance for anyone who was a slacker. Like the elder brother, the Pharisees and scribes were more concerned with what took place on the outside of a person than what was going on inside the person. Rules, regulations, and rituals were the most important items on their religious agenda. To my chagrin, I must admit that, for a long time, I had empathy for—and even defended—the elder brother. I was a hard worker, and I had no tolerance for layabouts.

There are so many within the community of faith who work hard at keeping rules and regulations. If we are not careful, we can develop our own clipboard list of what we should do and should not do—and then we expect others to adhere to the same. This was precisely the position of the Pharisees and the scribes. This was why they could relate to the elder brother and had no tolerance for the prodigals.

In no way am I insinuating that rules and regulations are inherently bad. They are not. However, when we judge a person as being in right standing with the heavenly Father because of their rule-keeping abilities, we are skating on thin ice.

Later on, Jesus said to the same audience of synagogue leaders:

> You like to appear righteous in public, but God knows your hearts. What this world honors is detestable in the sight of God. (Luke 16:15 NLT)

This same spirit is hanging heavy over the family of faith today. We give more attention to—and place more importance on—how we conduct ourselves publicly than we do privately. Personality is who we are publicly, but character is who we are privately.

The walkaway son shared his father's home, but he did not share his father's heart.

CHAPTER  SEVEN

# THE LOST SOUL

---

## There Is No Celebration

The purpose behind Jesus telling the story about a lost sheep, a lost piece of silver, and a lost son is for us to know what God the Father thinks about us, how God sees us, and how God feels about us. There is a great celebration in heaven when a person comes to the Father with a broken spirit and a contrite heart (Psalm 51:17 NKJV). He places them into his forever family. Nothing excites our heavenly Father more than seeing his family grow. The birth of spiritual babies is a special moment, and it will always be celebrated by the Father. All the angels in glory join in.

Jesus tells another story about a poor man and a rich man: a beggar clothed in rags and a rich man clothed in royalty. This story is about a lost soul. A lost soul is out of place for time and for eternity. There is no celebration in heaven. God the Father never takes any delight when a person dies out of place because they will be separated from him for eternity. I would imagine that heaven is strangely quiet when this happens.

Many people see this story about a lost soul as a parable just like the one Jesus told about the sheep, the silver, and the son. I'm not convinced it is because Jesus uses the proper name, Lazarus, in this story. Don't confuse this Lazarus with the brother of Mary and Martha (John 11:1–44 NKJV). They are not one and the same.

We are told that this Lazarus is a beggar. From what Jesus said, he had to have assistance each day to get where he needed to be so he could beg for his food. He was laid at the rich man's gate, hoping to scrounge some crumbs that fell from his table. Lazarus looked like a beggar. He begged like a beggar. I'm sure he smelled like one too.

The beggar was destitute, and he suffered from a skin disease. He was covered in sores. The stray dogs, in their search of table scraps, would lick his open wounds as he lay helpless at the rich man's gate. The dogs showed more compassion for Lazarus than the rich man who lived inside the gate. Life is tough!

Inside the gate was a different scene. The rich man dined sumptuously every day on the finest cuisine and drank expensive wine. He had the best of everything: clothes, home, food, and servants. Anything he wanted was at his beck and call. I'm sure he bathed on a regular basis and smelled pretty good. There's no doubt he had access to the best medical care. Life is good!

Materially speaking, these two men have nothing in common. Their physical conditions are diametrically opposite. Lazarus was trying to catch a few scraps that fell from the world's table, and the rich man seemingly has the world by the tail. Lazarus nibbled crumbs outside in the streets with the stray dogs, and the rich man dined inside with his royal guests. Lazarus's goal was to survive the day. The rich man lived by the philosophy of get all you can, can all you get, and then sit on the can. On second thought, maybe these two men have more in common than it appears.

## A Change Is Coming

Shelves in bookstores are overflowing with how-to books. You can find a book on just about any subject you can imagine—and some you can't imagine. You can even buy a book telling you "how to die." Keep your credit card in your wallet. Don't waste your money on buying how-to books about dying. You are old enough to die as soon as you are born. You will do it right the first time. Death is common for every person. We will leave this world holding onto the same thing we came into the world holding: nothing. We were born naked, and we will die the same.

Jesus tells us that both men died. Life's playing field was made obvious. It was level. Lazarus was immediately carried by the angels to Abraham's bosom. This is a phrase taken from the practice of reclining at meals. The head of one person would lay on the bosom of another. It speaks of intimacy and friendship:

> Now there was leaning on Jesus' *bosom* one of His disciples [John], whom Jesus loved. (John 13:23 NKJV; emphasis added)

The Jews had no doubt Abraham was in paradise, and saying that Lazarus was in his bosom was saying that he was ushered into heaven when he died. Abraham's bosom is a common term among Jews. It means to be in the most favored place. It carries the idea of a great feast, and Abraham is the host.

This is an incredible transition, isn't it? Lazarus went from begging for scraps on the streets to feasting with Father Abraham. He went from abject poverty to paradise. Lazarus did not go to heaven because he was poor. His status in this world had nothing to do with it. It was because the Lord knew his name:

> To him the doorkeeper opens, and the sheep hear his voice, and *he calls his own sheep by name* and leads them out. (John 10:3 NKJV; emphasis added)

I think we are getting an inkling as to why Jesus used the proper name: Lazarus.

Death came knocking on the rich man's door, and Jesus tells us that he was buried. That means there was a memorial service held in his honor. I'm sure the service held in his memory was extravagant. No expense was too great. He was a rich man. Remember that death comes for the rich as well as the poor. Death comes once per person:

> [And] As it is appointed for men to die once, but after this the judgment. (Hebrews 9:27 NKJV)

While the celebration service was going on for the rich man here on earth, the real man was experiencing torment in Hades. To make his suffering even greater, he could see Lazarus in Abraham's bosom. The script had flipped. Lazarus was feasting inside with Abraham, and the rich man was thirsting outside the gate. However, there were no dogs to lick his wounds. The rich man's attention was focused on the person he found easy to overlook before: the man sitting outside his gate and begging for bread crumbs.

The rich man did not go to Hades, a place of torment, because he was rich. It was because the Lord did not know him as one of his sheep (John 10:3 NKJV). The rich man was now the beggar:

> Father Abraham, have mercy on me, and send Lazarus that he may dip the tip of his finger in water and cool my tongue; for I am tormented in this flame. (Luke 16:24 NKJV)

The rich man had become the poor man, and he was begging for basic life sustenance: water. Expensive wine was not on his wish list. A drink of cool water was what he begged for: "Father Abraham, please have mercy on me. I beg you, send Lazarus to help me. Have him dip the tip of his finger in water and touch my tongue. I'm tormented by these flames." Isn't it a little ironic that he was asking for help from the one he refused to help? Lazarus would have settled for crumbs from the rich man's table, and now he was feasting in heaven. The rich man who feasted on the best food and drink on earth was asking for a fingertip of water to cool his tongue as he was tormented in Hades. The man from whom Lazarus begged for bread crumbs was now begging Lazarus for a smidgen of water.

The answer he gets is this: "Son, remember" (Luke 16:25 NKJV). The rich man had been separated from God for eternity and would have his forever memory intact—remembering the times when he could have made better decisions, helped more people, been kinder, and surrendered his life to God. Now, it's too late. There will be no do-overs.

Where we spend eternity will be determined by our decision to accept Christ or reject Christ while we are living on this earth. Once we close our eyes in death, our eternal fate is sealed. We will be with God or separated from God. There will be a celebration—or there will be no celebration. Heaven will never celebrate those who die out of place:

> [God] desires all men to be saved and to come to the knowledge of the truth. (1 Timothy 2:4 NKJV)

Our heavenly Father and his angels never celebrate a lost soul:

> But Abraham said, Son, remember that in your lifetime you received your good things, and likewise Lazarus evil things; but now he is comforted and you are tormented. (Luke 16:25 NKJV)

The rich man was reminded that his life on earth was filled with plenty. He wanted for nothing. Anything he dreamed of having he was able to purchase. He could quench his thirst, eat the finest foods, sleep in a comfortable bed, hobnob with the social elite, and dress in the latest fashions. He could also keep the street urchins off of his property—like Lazarus—but there are some things money can't buy. He was beginning to experience the reality of this statement.

## A Person's Eternal Destination Is Determined before They Die

A person can play now and pay later—or they can pay now and play later. The *now* is temporal. The *later* is permanent. Every person is given this choice. When we close our eyes in death, the decision we made is sealed forever. There will be no second chances and no starting over. Reality begins on the other side of death's door:

> And beside all this, between us and you there is a great gulf fixed, so that those who want to pass from here to you cannot, nor can those from there pass to us. (Luke 16:26 NKJV)

## The Rich Man's Concern for His Lost Brothers

The rich man had concerns for his five brothers since they were in the same spiritual boat as he was:

> Then he said, "I beg you therefore, father, that you would send him to my father's house, for *I have five brothers*, that he may testify to them, that they also come to this place of torment." (Luke 16:27–28 NKJV; emphasis added)

I find it interesting that he didn't show much concern for others before his death. He'd had a change of mind, but it was too late. Think about how sad that was. One brother was in hell, and five were on their way to hell. It was a sad state of affairs.

I've heard a few people in my time say in a smirky and flippant way that they don't mind going to hell because they will have plenty of company. What this rich man asks for doesn't sound like he wants company, especially his own family. Again, reality is on the other side of death's door.

At face value, this seems like a reasonable request. This man has five brothers who have chosen to play over pay. Unless they are warned about what awaits them on the other side of death's door, his reality will become theirs.

> Abraham said to him, "They have Moses and the prophets; let them hear them." And he said, "No, father Abraham; but if someone goes to them from the dead, they will repent." (Luke 16:29–30 NKJV)

The answer the rich man is given sounds a little cold when you first hear it. Can you imagine the impact it would make on his brothers if someone from the dead were to show up on their front porch and give them a firsthand report on the reality of hell? Surely, if someone came to his brothers from the pit of hell and shared their testimony, all of them would repent.

It's Sunday morning, and the service is in full swing. All of a sudden, an individual walks to the pulpit and starts sharing their testimony. "I have come to tell you that hell is real. I've been there, and I must return after I give you this report. Jesus told you about the rich man and Lazarus. Your pastor has preached on it for years. God wants you to know that hell is a real place, and if you go there, you will be confined in torment for eternity. You cannot blame God if you end up there. He has warned you many times. The only way to escape is to accept and receive his Son Jesus Christ as your Lord and Savior. The Lord does not want anyone to die and be separated from him for eternity. You will not be given a second chance after you die. Believe me. I must go now."

Before this individual can finish giving their report, many people within the congregation have already dialed 911 on their cell phones. "We have an insane person here, and we need help—now!" The sirens from the ambulance and police cars wail as they arrive to take this individual to get psychiatric help, but this person is nowhere to be found.

We have been given the written Word. Moses and the prophets wrote about life after death. Where a person spends eternity will depend on their decision to place their trust in God through Jesus Christ before they die. If a person will not believe what the Word of God says about life after death, they will not believe if someone comes back from the dead with a message of warning:

> But he said to him, "If they do not hear Moses and the prophets, neither will they be persuaded though one rise form the dead." (Lue 16:31 NKJV)

## The Second Death: A Place of Eternal Torment

Skeptics and critics who attack the legitimacy of the Word of God are quick to point out that Jesus did not use the word *hell* in this story about the rich man and Lazarus. He uses the word *Hades*, which means *grave*. It is not the lake of fire burning with brimstone that many preachers talk about. And this is true. Their argument is that since the word Hades means grave, once a person dies and goes to the grave, that is the end of the story. Life ends for them. They forget—or have overlooked—the fact that the rich man was in torment in Hades. He begged for mercy:

> I am tormented in this flame. (Luke 15:23–24 NKJV)

Even though Hades does mean grave, it is a place of torment for the unbeliever. It is the first death for them. A second death, a place of eternal fire and brimstone, is coming.

When an unbeliever dies, they go to a place of torment. In the story Jesus tells about the rich man and Lazarus, he calls this place Hades. This is the first death the Word of God talks about. There will be a second death: a place of eternal torment. Hades is not the final destiny for unbelievers; Gehenna is.

In the book of Revelation, the writer talks about the end of time—not of eternity, but the end of time. When Jesus returns to this earth, the beast and the one who deceived people with miracles of deception (the false prophet) will be captured and cast into the lake of fire:

> These two were cast alive into the lake of fire burning with brimstone. (Revelation 19:20 NKJV)

## The devil will also have his day of reckoning:

> The devil, who deceived them, was cast into the lake of fire and brimstone where the beast and the false prophet are. And they will be tormented day and night forever and ever. (Revelation 20:10 NKJV)

Those who die without Christ will stand before God at the white throne of judgement. They will be raised from Hades, judged for their sins and rejection of Christ, and then cast into the lake of fire:

> Then Death and Hades [the grave] were cast into the lake of fire. *This is the second death.* (Revelation 20:14 NKJV; emphasis added)

> But the cowardly, unbelieving, abominable, murderers, sexually immoral, sorcerers, idolaters, and all liars shall have their part in the lake which burns with fire and brimstone, *which is the second death.* (Revelation 21:8 NKJV; emphasis added)

Hell was not created for humanity. It was created for the devil and his imps. However, a person will find their eternal destiny in hell if they refuse God's invitation to life through his Son, Jesus Christ. A person never goes to hell because of God's badness. No one has ever been sent—or ever will be sent—to hell. A person goes to hell because of their own choice to reject God's invitation to life. No one can ever legitimately blame God for their eternal punishment. Their choice is made on this side of death's door:

> And the Spirit and the bride say, "Come!" And let him who hears say, "Come!" And let him who thirsts come. Whoever desires, let him take the water of life freely. (Revelation 22:17 NKJV)

God is good, and whatever he is, he is completely. Since he is good, he is completely good. Never forget that heaven does not celebrate over a lost soul. God desires everyone to be saved.

## The Heart of This Story

Worldly possessions may help you get by in this life, but they are of no benefit in the afterlife. Time spent on this side of death's door is temporal. Life on the other side of death's door is eternal. Where we end up will be determined while we are on this temporal side. God will not make this decision for us. He has given us free will. His desire is for everyone to accept his personal invitation to spend eternity with him. He wants us to celebrate together. Invitations to the party in the Lord's house have been mailed—in the person of Jesus Christ. Where we spend eternity will be our personal choice. Choose wisely. Play now and pay later—or pay now and play later. The ball is in your court.

A person does not go to heaven because they are poor or because they are rich. Where a person spends eternity will not be decided by the possessions they have, but in whom they have believed. Jesus said, "Let not your heart be troubled; *you believe in God, believe also in Me*" (John 14:1 NKJV; emphasis added). Believing in God makes a person a Deist, and believing in Christ makes a person a Christian. Only Christians will spend eternity with God when they close their eyes in death on this side of death's door.

Someone might think that all is well with their soul since they believe in God, but they might not be sure about Jesus. Here's what the Word of God says about this:

> Who is a liar but he who denies that Jesus is the Christ? He is antichrist who denies the Father and the Son. *Whoever denies the Son does not have the Father either; he who acknowledges the Son has the Father also.* (1 John 2:22–23 NKJV; emphasis added)

> And this is the testimony: that God has given us eternal life and this life is in His Son. He who has the Son has life; he who does not have the Son of God does not have life. These things I have written to you who believe in the name of the Son of God, that you may know that you have eternal life, and that you may continue to believe in the name of the Son of God. (1 John 5:11–13 NKJV; emphasis added)

You can hear the gavel of God slamming down on his sacred desk, followed by these words: "This case has been settled."

Lazarus lay at the rich man's gate every day. Having a gate entrance to his home tells us it was quite a place. In that day and time, a gated entrance was not common. Only the rich and powerful had property large enough to justify having a fence with a gate. Lazarus was laid at this man's gate entrance every day by someone or several people so he could beg for table scraps. Every day, he went unnoticed by everyone behind the gate except for the stray dogs that came by to lick his wounds. It turns out the only stray was the rich man who lived behind the gate.

Physical looks can be deceiving. It appears as if the rich man is in the right place, but when it is all said and done, he ends up in the wrong place. To be lost is to be out of place. A lost soul will be out of place for an eternity, and there is no celebration when a soul dies out of place. Just because someone may be doing well physically and materially, it does not mean they are doing well spiritually. Having a lot of worldly stuff is not what God uses to measure a healthy soul.

Being rich and being wealthy are not necessarily synonymous terms. The major difference between being rich and being wealthy is duration. What a wealthy person has is sustainable, and they will always be wealthy no matter what happens to them in life. Riches on the other hand, last for a short period of time.

The rich man in this story enjoyed what he had, but what he had was not sustainable. He lost it all and ended up poor for an eternity. Lazarus struggled with poverty while he lived on this earth, but he died wealthy and will enjoy his wealth for eternity. What distinguishes wealth from riches is a healthy soul:

> Beloved, I pray that you may prosper in all things and be in health, just as your soul prospers. (3 John 1:2 NKJV)

True sustainable wealth is a healthy soul. Death will determine if a person is rich or wealthy. The rich man was rich, but he was not wealthy. He lost it all at his death. Lazarus was not rich. He was very poor, but he became very wealthy when he died.

CHAPTER  EIGHT

# THIS IS OUR STORY

---

## Sandals: One Size Fits All

The story that Jesus was telling the Pharisees and scribes ended with the father reminding his pouting eldest son that celebrating the return of his brother was the right thing to do:

> It is right that we should make merry and be glad,
> for your brother was dead and is alive again, and
> was lost and is found. (Luke 15:32 NKJV)

Celebrating the return of a prodigal was very offensive to the elder brother. He was more interested in justice than mercy. Don't you dare mention grace.

It is easy to get so caught up in this story that we forget why Jesus was telling it. The Pharisees and scribes were upset with Jesus because he had the audacity to meet with sinners. The lowest of the low and the down-and-out were attracted to Jesus. He was kind and accepting, and these self-righteous religious fanatics could not accept this. Jesus wanted everyone to know that God the Father will receive anyone no matter where they may be in their story. Even though the

Lord hates sin, he loves the sinner—and the sinners knew it. It was the synagogue's self-righteous ones who did not believe it.

The story ends in a way that leaves us in a state of wonder. Did the two sons reconcile their relationship as brothers? Did the youngest son find his place in his father's home? Did he share his father's heart? Did the oldest son come to grips with the bitterness he had toward his youngest brother? Did he get over the jealously he had for his brother because his father celebrated his return after he had wasted his livelihood on riotous living? The way Jesus ended the story leaves us with a plethora of unanswered questions.

Could Jesus have purposely left us hanging? Is this really our story? Has Jesus left the story up to us to complete? If this is the case, the ball is now in our court. What will we do? We can't go back to the beginning and change our stories, but we can start where we are and end our stories well. It is a choice that only we can make. Choose your sandals wisely.

There are four pairs of sandals in this story. We have the sandals of the Pharisees and scribes, the elder brother, the prodigal, and the sandals of the father. One size will fit us all. It is our choice which ones we wear. It is possible to wear all four pairs on any given day.

## Tight-Fit Sandals

The sandals of the Pharisees and scribes are tight-fitting sandals. There is very little wiggle room in these snug-fit sandals. The people who wear these shoes are more concerned with religious protocol than they are with having a personal relationship with the Father. When you slip these sandals on your feet, you become very judgmental and condemning. A clipboard of dos-and-don'ts clipped to your belt becomes the most important accessory in your wardrobe. When we choose to wear these tight-fitting religious sandals, we become critical and judgmental of those who are not living up to our list. We don't like certain people, especially those who do not kowtow to our set of rules, and it upsets us when we hear that God receives sinners.

The Pharisees and scribes were not always bad people. At one time, their hearts were in the right place. All they wanted was for the people of God to know the Law, love the Law, and live their lives according to the Law. To accomplish this, they came up with rules that would help people in their efforts to live lives that were pleasing to God. It didn't take long before things began to veer off course, and the rules to keep the law became more important than the law.

When a construction crew builds a structure, they often construct temporary scaffolding on the outside or inside of the building. This scaffolding is used by the workers to give them access to their workspace. The workers can stand or sit on it when they are working at a height above the floor or ground. The scaffolding is intended to be a temporary, moveable platform. Once construction is complete, the scaffolding is removed.

This is kind of what the Pharisees had in mind when they came up with rules to help people keep the law. The rules were meant to be scaffolding. If you follow this rule, you will find it easier to obey a particular law. It didn't take long before the scaffolding became more important than the Word of God. They never removed the scaffolding. People were striving to be perfect on the outside by observing the rules, but they remained flawed on the inside. It really doesn't matter if a person's heart is in it. That's not the important thing—doing is. The Pharisees began to demand others to follow the same rituals, rules, and regulations as they were. If a person refused, they were to be rejected and ostracized. To the Pharisees, doing became more important than being. Religion tells you what to do and how to do it, but it can't help you do it.

This is why the Pharisees and scribes were so upset with Jesus. He didn't follow the rules. Every law keeper knows you don't fellowship with sinners—and you certainly don't eat with them. If you do, you are openly declaring that you accept them This is unacceptable to someone who chooses to wear these tight-fitting sandals:

And the Pharisees and scribes *complained*, saying, "This Man [Jesus] receives sinners and eats with them." (Luke 15:2 NKJV; emphasis added)

There is only one way a person can go if they submit to a system of dos and don'ts: an exaggerated sense of one's own importance. Our church buildings are filled on a weekly basis with modern-day Pharisees and scribes. These people are religious rule followers. Religion tells you what to do and how to do it. Grace tells you who you are. When you know who you are, no one has to tell you what to do. You know.

## Loose-Fit Sandals

The Pharisees and scribes wore tight-fitting sandals. The prodigal chose the loose-fitting kind. He wore running shoes. These running sandals are large, wide, and know no boundaries. These shoes will take you farther than you want to go. They will keep you longer than you want to stay, and they will cost you more than you want to pay. These sandals look good, but they have weak soles and will easily give in to temptation. They look good on your feet, but they cannot provide the comfort they advertise. These shoes are designed for rebellious, self-centered runaways. When you see a person wearing these shoes, they will probably be wearing a T-shirt with "Me, Me, Me" stenciled on it. Life is all about them.

Prodigals do not want limitations, barriers, or boundaries in their lives. They want an open range so they can graze freely. Their theme song is "Don't Fence Me In," a song from 1934 written by Robert Fletcher and Cole Porter and sung by Bing Crosby. Submission is not in their vocabulary. Someone with a prodigal bent does not want the restrictions of home life. They want to call their own shots and live the wild life.

Having boundaries is actually a healthy thing. Back in the

day, cattle grazed freely by the thousands. There were no fences or restrictions to impede their ability to roam and graze. This worked well until much of the range was overgrazed, and more and more settlers moved in to set up their homesteads.

In 1870, barbed wire was introduced to confine cattle to designated grazing areas. Many range wars were fought over barbed wire and the restrictions it created. In the long run, fencing proved to be the best thing for settlers, the grazing areas, and for the cattle. The cattle could roam free and graze within the boundaries created by the fencing. Cattle sometimes broke through the barbed wire, causing damage to personal property, grazing areas, and themselves, but it was not nearly as many as when there were no boundaries.

When the prodigal said to his father, "'Father, give me the portion of goods that falls to me.' So he divided to them his livelihood" (Luke 15:12 NKJV), he was in essence saying, "I'm tired of being fenced in by you. I want my freedom to graze in the faraway country." The prodigal son did not want the restrictions of his homelife. He wanted his freedom so he could call his own shots, do his own thing, and answer to no one. We know how that worked out, don't we?

I was sitting in the stands with hundreds, if not a couple of thousand people, watching our high school football team play a very important district game. We were on our own twenty-yard line. The quarterback made a quick pitch to our running back. This dude had some wheels. When he made it to the corner, he turned upfield and ran for an eighty-yard touchdown—untouched. The stands went berserk. We were all high-fiving, glad-handing, and screaming our lungs out. All of a sudden, a quiet hush swept across the stadium. At the twenty-yard line, there was a yellow flag. You could hear a low groan emitting from the stands. Our running back's toe had barely crossed the chalk on the sideline. He had stepped out of bounds. He had transgressed the boundaries of the playing field. The score was taken off of the scoreboard, and the ball was replaced at the mark of the transgression. This great running back had those yards removed from his stats as well. He was penalized, the team was penalized, the fans were disappointed. Why? He stepped over the boundary line of the playing field, which is in violation of the rules of the game of football. The game must be played within the designated markers; otherwise, there will be a penalty for failing to do so.

Loose-fit sandals are good for one thing: stepping out of bounds. When we wear these sandals, we are saying the rules of life don't apply to us. We may be children of the Father, but since we have a free will, we can make poor choices that have consequences. These consequences affect us, and they can touch those closest to us as well. Choose your sandals wisely.

## Custom-Fit Sandals

Custom-fit sandals were the shoes of choice by the elder brother. He was the walkaway son: the son who shared his father's home but not his father's heart. Since his sandals were custom-made, I'm sure E. B. was branded on the side of them: Elder Brother.

The elder brother's heart was exposed when he talked to his father:

> All these years I've slaved for you and never once refused to do a single thing you told me to. And in all that time you never gave me even one young goat for a feast with my friends. Yet when this son of yours comes back after squandering your money on prostitutes, you celebrate by killing the fatted calf. (Luke 15:29 NLTV)

His heart did not correspond with his hands. It is obvious why more prodigals don't come home. They don't want to deal with the elder brothers. The elder brothers are harder to please than the father.

Pay close attention to what the elder brother said to his father: All these years I have been slaving for you (Luke 15:29 NKJV). The elder brother did work hard, which is why most people tend to side with him. We can see his hard work, and it is impressive. He is to be commended. What we can't see is his heart. He did the right thing, but he had the wrong attitude. The elder brother lived like a slave; therefore, he could not think like a son. He was working hard to get what he already had: his birthright privileges.

It is apparent the elder son had a short-term memory problem. He never refused to do anything his father asked him to do "in his entire lifetime" (Luke 15:29 NKJV). I find that difficult to believe. Is it possible for a boy to grow into manhood and never once disobey his father? Maybe his jealousy and anger over the treatment his younger brother was receiving caused him to have a momentary mental lapse. Had he forgotten the times he *sluffed off* and did not do what he was supposed to do or told his father he had done? These custom-sandal guys have a way of conveniently forgetting facts, especially when they don't fit their narrative.

His father killing the fatted calf inflamed his anger toward his younger brother—and for his father. If it had been left up to him, he would have sent his brother packing down the road or had him stoned to death. He probably would have leaned toward the latter. The elder brother complained that he had never been given a goat so he could have a party with his friends. If I were interrogating this young man, I would ask him to give me the names of five people on his friends list. I would wager the farm that he couldn't name one—not even another elder brother. Elder brothers don't like other elder brothers.

Because of the disdain he had for his brother, he refused to acknowledge him as his brother. Instead, he said, "This son of yours" (Luke 15:30 NKJV). Elder brothers are like that. They don't like to see the *undeserved* treated with kindness and grace. Punishment? Yes. Grace? No!

He reminded his father that the prodigal was his son and not his brother—as if the father had forgotten. As far as he was concerned, the moment the prodigal ran away from home in his loose-fitting sandals, he was no longer considered a part of the family. He had lost all rights as a family member. Blood is not thicker than water to an elder brother.

Elder brothers are quick to expose the faults and sins of others:

> When this son of yours comes back after squandering your money on prostitutes, you celebrate by killing the fattened calf. (Luke 15:30 NKJV)

I have an immediate red flag. How did the elder brother know how his brother spent his money? He sure didn't get this information from his father. The father never mentioned his youngest son's past. This is what people do who wear elder brother custom-fit sandals. They expose the sins and shortcomings of others. They refuse to give others what they themselves want to be given: grace. The elder brother exposed his brother's sin:

> And above all things have fervent love for one another, for "*love will cover a multitude of sins.*" (1 Peter 4:8 NKJV; emphasis added)

The only person an elder brother loves is themselves.

## Grace-Fit Sandals

In this story, both sons are headed home to a waiting father. After a hard day's work, the elder son is coming home from the field in his custom-fit sandals. By his own words, he has been slaving in the hot fields for his father. He never left home physically, but his heart had left a long time ago—along with his respect and compassion for his father. Even though his heart was somewhere else, he continued to share his father's home. He was all work and no play.

After a season of self-indulgent living, the youngest son was coming home from the faraway country, shoeless. He had lost his loose-fitting play shoes. The prodigal son had learned one thing: payday might not be every Friday, but there will be a payday. You play, you pay. He was all play and no work.

Even though both boys were their father's sons and had shared his homes for years, they didn't know their father's heart. Since they didn't really know him, they were not sure what their father thought about them, how he saw them, or how he felt about them. They were both about to find out.

The father met both sons wearing his sandals—sandals of grace. When he saw his runaway son coming home, he ran to him. He grabbed his son in his arms and loved on him. His son was back where he belonged, and that filled the heart of the father with great joy. You would expect some sort of reprimand, but there was none. After all, his son had turned his back on him and the family. He had squandered the livelihood his father had worked so hard to accumulate. At least he could have been placed on probation for a period of time. What if he pulled the same stunt again? But there was no lecture, no sermon, and not even an "I told you so." What mattered to the father was that his son was back where he belonged.

The father met his walkaway son with the same spirit and compassion that he had met his runaway son with. When the elder brother was approaching the house, after a hard day's work in the field, he could hear the celebration that was going on. The news about his brother being home and the party in his honor made him angry, and he refused to go inside. The father went out to him. He did not preach a sermon to his son or lecture him about why celebrating the return of his brother was the right thing to do. Wearing sandals of grace, the father went outside and met his son who was wearing his law sandals. Grace and law met face-to-face.

The elder brother seized the opportunity to vent all of his pent-up frustration and anger that was harbored in his heart toward his brother and his father. After spilling his guts about how he felt about his runaway brother—and how ludicrous it was for his father to throw a party in his honor—the father addressed him as his "son." He wanted his legalistic son to know they were still a family. The father showered the elder son with the same compassion that he lavished on his youngest son.

## The Heart of This Parable

The heart of God has not changed. What he was yesterday, he is today. What he is today, he will be tomorrow. God did not say he was or that he will be. He said, "I Am" (Exodus 3:14 NKJV). He will receive any and all who come to him because he is still wearing sandals of grace. Those who work hard, thinking they can earn their way to the Father, or those who work hard, trying to keep their position as sons, and even those who have thrown caution to the wind and are reaping the consequences from their choices are received with welcoming arms by the Father. There will be no lectures, sermons, or probation, but there will be a big celebration in the heavenly realm:

> And the Spirit and the bride say, "Come!" And let him who hears say, "Come!" And let him who thirsts come. Whoever desires, let him take the water of life freely. (Revelation 22:17 NKJV)

It is so easy to get caught up in what Jesus was saying and miss why he was saying it. What does Jesus want us to know by telling this parable? The father's response to both of his sons answered some questions most people wrestle with: What does the Father think about me? How does the Father see me? How does the Father feel about me? Jesus leaves us with no doubt to these questions by telling this parable about the sheep, the silver, and the sons. We are loved unconditionally by our heavenly Father, and he always has us on his mind:

> How precious are your thoughts about me, O God
> they cannot be numbered! I can't even count them;
> they outnumber the grains of sand! And when
> I wake up, you are still there. (Psalm 139:17–18
> NLTV)

There is no shortage of robes, rings, sandals, or fatted calves in the Father's house. He is always looking for the returning prodigals, as well as the hardworking, self-righteous, religious legalists:

> You [God] crown the year with Your goodness,
> and your paths drip with abundance. (Psalm 65:11
> NKJV)

It is impossible for anyone to stray so far away that it is impossible for them to be welcomed home by the Father. His arms are always ready to embrace the repentant sinner, the up-and-out, and the down-and-out. You are *always* in his thoughts! He said he would never leave us or forsake us (Hebrews 13:5 NKJV). That means if he loved us yesterday when we were lovable, he will love us today when we are unlovable. He never changes. We are always welcome in the Father's arms and in the Father's house.

The chorus to Christopher and Lynda Hylton's "He Never Left Me" encapsulates the heart of the Father for all of humanity:

> He never left me, though I turned my back on Him
> Living in a world of sin, trying to *run away* again.
> He never left me, when I chose to *walk away*.
> Even when I couldn't pray, He never left me.

If you are a runaway or a walkaway, the Father will welcome you home with open arms.

# CHAPTER NINE

# WHAT GOD THINKS ABOUT US

## How He Sees Us and How He Feels About Us

Until we change our thinking, we will always recycle our experiences. The prodigal son could not live like a son because he thought like a slave. The elder brother lived like a slave because he thought like a slave. Both sons did not know what their father thought about them, how he saw them, or how he felt about them. They were judging their father's feelings toward them on the basis of how they thought and felt.

The community of faith is experiencing an incalculable number of runaways and walkaways because of how they think. Many want to be restored to their rightful place as children of God, but they are not convinced they will be received with unconditional love if they were to come home. They fear the lectures, the sermons, the "I told you so," or the probation that may be awaiting them if they come home.

> But *God demonstrated His own love toward us,* in
> that while we were still sinners, Christ died for us.
> (Romans 5:8 NKJV; emphasis added)

God demonstrated (put on display) his love for a lost and dying world by sending his Son, Jesus Christ, to die on the cross for us—while we were still in a sinning state. He did not wait until we cleaned up our acts to demonstrate such incredible love. This far exceeds our human ability to grasp.

Let's place this verse within its context so we can get the full impact of what Paul is saying to the Christians who lived in Rome:

> When we were utterly helpless, Christ came at just
> the right time and died for us sinners. Now, most
> people would not be willing to die for an upright
> person, though someone might perhaps be willing
> to die for a person who is especially good. But God
> showed his great love for us by sending Christ to die
> for us while we were still sinners. (Romans 5:6–8
> NLTV)

This is amazing love, but this is exactly what the Word of God says: "God is love" (1 John 4:8 NKJV).

The enemy has convinced most people that God is a distant deity who is unapproachable, inaccessible, and unavailable to the average person. He is viewed as a Comic Cop by the majority of people in the religious world—even though they have no empirical evidence to validate this belief. They are convinced that God is always on the lookout for sinner speeders and law violators because he gets some sort of twisted pleasure out of punishing them. This is so diametrically opposed to the heart of God.

The parable of the prodigal son in Luke 15 disproves this theological construct. Jesus wants us to know that every person is valuable and loved by God. God demonstrated this by sending his

Son, Jesus Christ, to die for us long before we wanted anything to do with him. I would call this a high risk on God's part:

> For God so loved the world that He gave His only begotten Son, that whoever believes in Him should not perish but have everlasting life. (John 3:16 NKJV)

God is love, and what does love do? Love gives. This verse reveals the intensity of the love that God has for us—for God *so loved* the world.

Jesus paid a high price for our low living:

> For He (God) made Him (Jesus) who knew no sin to be sin for us, that we might become the righteousness of God in Him. (2 Corinthians 5:21 NKJV)

Read this verse slowly and allow the Spirit of God to write it indelibly in your soul. Let me give you my version of this verse. "What I was, Jesus was made, so I could be what he is."

Jesus never sinned. He was made sin for you. And this happened before you wanted anything to do with him. Jesus died for you while you were still in your sinning condition. Jesus was made what I was, so that I could become what he is. This is liberating: "As he is, so are we in this world" (1 John 4:17 NKJV). This is the truth that sets us free *from* sin—not free *to* sin. Are you beginning to get a picture of what God thinks about you? God is not mad at you. He is madly in love with you.

## Characters in the Prodigal Son Story

The man who went to search for the one lost sheep represents Jesus, the Good Shepherd. It was the shepherd who went in search for the lost sheep:

> And Jesus said to him, "Today salvation has come to this house, because he also is a son of Abraham; for the *Son of Man has come to seek and to save that which is lost.*" (Luke 19:9–10 NKJV; emphasis added)

The woman represents the Holy Spirit. She lit a lamp, the lamp of truth, and searched the house from the inside for the one lost piece of silver:

> But God has revealed [uncovered] them to us through His Spirit. For *the Spirit searches all things,* yes, the deep things of God. (1 Corinthians 2:10 NKJV; emphasis added)

The father in this parable represents our heavenly Father. He is the main character of this story. Pay close attention to how he interacts with and treats both of his sons. This will tell you what God thinks about you. God's heart is full of grace, not vengeance.

There is an unfounded fear within the community of faith that emphasizing the love and grace of God will give people a license to sin. People have sinned since Genesis 3 without a license. Knowing how much God loves you will not create in you a desire to sin. God's love and grace changes your "want to." You don't want to sin. The desire to sin is taken away by the love and grace of God:

> Either way, *Christ's love controls us* [constrains us]. Since we believe that Christ died for all, we also believe that we have all died to our old life. (2 Corinthians 5:14 NLT; emphasis added)

The father in this parable showed the same affection for both of his sons. He loves the self-indulgent sinner (youngest son), and he loves the self-righteous sinner (elder brother). Don't forget what Paul said in his letter to the Roman Christians: God put on public display his love for every person, the self-indulgent and the self-righteous, by sending Jesus to die on the cross for the whole world.

> There is no fear in love; but *perfect love casts out fear*, because fear involves torment. But he who fears has not been made perfect in love. We love Him because He first loved us. (1 John 4:18–19 NKJV; emphasis added)

When we begin to grasp how much God loves us—no matter what—we will no longer be afraid of our missteps causing him to love us less:

> [And may you] be able to comprehend with all the saints what is the width and length and depth and height—to know the love of Christ which passes knowledge; that you may be filled with all the fullness of God. (Ephesians 3:18–19 NKJV)

God's love is so phenomenal that we mortals cannot fully grasp it. Our love for one another often depends on the behavior of the person we are trying to love. God's love for us is not. His love for us is unadulterated, unmixed, unconditional, and fully available to every repentant sinner. His love for us is not conditioned on what we do. He loves us because we are his creation. What God did by sending his Son to take our place on the cross—to bear our sin, to die our death—is beyond understanding. The beauty is that we don't have to understand it. All we have to do is accept it.

God wants us to know how much he loves us because when we do, we cannot help but love him back. I am possibly the most fortunate man on the face of the earth. I have one incredible soul mate covenant partner in my wife, Betty Ann Kniffen. I have never been loved by anyone on this earth like she loves me. Her love for me has not been with words only, though she never fails to tell me how much she loves me. Her actions have validated her words. When I share our covenant relationship at marriage conferences or at men's retreats, I get that "I'm having a hard time believing what you're saying" look. People who are not fortunate to have a great relationship with a spouse find it hard to believe that someone can have an incredible union.

In all the years that Betty Ann and I have been married, not once has she raised her voice to me. She has never given me the cold shoulder or the silent treatment. I have never been given the evil eye or "that look." Not once! For the first few years of our marriage, I expected the day would come when she would lose it and blow up. After all these years, she never has.

In all the years we've been together, I have come up with some genius ideas about all kinds of things—things to buy and business adventures—and my beloved has never shot down one of my ideas or belittled me. On numerous occasions, she has said, "I trust you." When she says that, I begin to pump the brakes. I don't want to do anything or make a decision that will adversely affect her or our marriage. Why? Because she trusts me.

God's love for us is far greater than any love we will find or share on this earth. He knows that if we begin to understand how much he loves us, we will not want to do anything or make decisions that will grieve the Holy Spirit. It is his love that constrains us from becoming the prodigal son or the elder brother. The main character in this story—and in our life stories—is the Father.

The elder brother represents the Jews: the Pharisees and scribes. Why did this story about lost sheep, lost silver, and a lost son rile them so much? Because they knew he was talking about them. This is why they ridiculed and mocked him. They also knew the younger brother represented the Gentiles—people they hated. There is no way God will accept these unclean infidels—much less celebrate when one of them comes to the Father.

The Jews hated the Gentiles. They considered them to be outcasts and scum. There is no way the father will receive Gentiles like the father welcomes the wayward son in Jesus's story. They do not have the right to be in the presence of the "law followers," and they certainly cannot be included as family members.

The elder brothers are the main obstacles standing between the prodigals and the father. More prodigals would come home if they did not have to deal with the elder brothers. They know these guys would not afford them any wiggle room. The religious elite demand strict adherence to the letter of the law. By the way, the law requires personal, perpetual perfection. The law requires you to be what it cannot help you be: perfect. No one can live up to what the Law demands, including the Pharisees and the scribes. They demanded from others what they could not do themselves: If you ever blow it, the chances are slim that you will ever be able to get back in the graces of the Father.

When the elder brother was having his moment with his father after coming home from a hard day's work in the fields, he would not admit the prodigal son was his brother. He said to his father, "This son of yours" (Luke 15:30 NKJV). In essence, he was saying, "Your prodigal son is not a part of my family." The Jews could not call a Gentile brother. No way.

The Pharisees and scribes had an openly hostile attitude toward Jesus. They were constantly looking for ways to silence him, discredit him, and even kill him. Why? Everything Jesus did was for the good of people. They even began to spread the false narrative that Jesus was possessed by demons and that the miracles he performed were from the power of Satan:

> And the scribes who came down from Jerusalem said, "He has Beelzebub," and, "By the ruler of the demons He casts out demons." (Mark 3:22 NKJV)

They wanted to silence him because he was draining their religious swamp. Their entire religious system was being undermined by his teachings.

There was another motivation behind their constant attempts to destroy Jesus. He had the audacity to claim he was God in the flesh. Jesus spoke to them as they were gathering up stones to take him out:

> "Many good works I have shown you from My Father. For which of those works do you stone Me?" The Jews answered Him, saying, "For a good work we do not stone You, but for blasphemy, and because You; being a Man, make Yourself God." (John 10:32–33 NKJV)

Are there any noticeable symptoms if a person has the elder brother syndrome? How do we know if we are wearing the elder brother sandals? When an individual is acting like an elder brother, they are usually oblivious to it. They either *can't* see it—or they *refuse* to see it. It's one or the other.

An elder brother enjoys playing the comparison game, always measuring themselves by others, and saying, "I may not be living up to the religious standard, but at least I'm not like so-and-so." They become resentful when others, especially the prodigals, are blessed. They did nothing to deserve it. An elder brother is quick to spot the flaws in others and is not hesitant to point them out. An elder brother has a difficult time when someone gets away with what they consider bad behavior. Deep down inside, an elder brother feels God owes them something. After all, they stayed home and continued to work hard. An elder brother works hard to attain what they already have.

There may be more elder brother symptoms in us than we realize. If left unchecked, it can metastasize into full-blown elder brother syndrome. A person who is acting like an elder brother may even leave the church by running away or walking away. It will always be someone else's fault too. It never crosses their minds that some have left the church because of them.

The younger brother represents the Gentiles. The Jews in biblical times saw the Gentiles as heathens, pagans, infidels, heretics, pagans, idolaters, and the list goes on. When Jesus talked about the youngest son going to a faraway country and spending his livelihood on prodigal living, I'm sure they all said, "Amen. That sounds just like a Gentile. He is out gallivanting when his elder brother (represents the Jews) stayed home and continued to work hard."

Their "amen" became "oh me" when Jesus talked about the prodigal returning home in repentance. Their phylacteries blew up when they heard how the father responded to this sinner son in grace and not the Law. They could not understand how the father could throw a huge party to celebrate his son's return. They thought, *Let's have a trial. He needs to get what he deserves.*

Jesus pushed them to the brink of insanity when he explained how the father lavished his wayward son with extravagant gifts. This son, who represents the Gentiles, found grace when he was not looking for it. He was willing to be a hired servant. The Jews were looking for grace, but they couldn't find it because they were trying to work for it: "All these years I have been slaving for you."

The apostle Paul was a Jew. He became what he was trying to eradicate: a Christian. He too was looking for righteousness (right standing with God) by keeping the Law. He worked hard, but he did not find what he was longing and searching for. He found grace on his way to Damascus to prosecute and persecute the people of the Way. Because of his life and experience, his words carry a lot of weight. Here is what he says about attaining righteousness:

> What shall we say then? That Gentiles (the prodigal son), who did not pursue righteousness, have attained to righteousness, even the righteousness of faith: but Israel (the elder son), pursuing the law of righteousness, has not attained to the law of righteousness. Why? Because they did not seek it by faith, but as it were, by the works of the law. For they stumbled at that stumbling stone. (Romans 9:30–32 NKJV)

What Paul says is mind-blowing. Read these verses again from a different translation:

> Even though the Gentiles were not trying to follow
> God's standards, they were made right with God.
> And it was by faith that this took place. But he
> people of Israel, who tried so hard to get right with
> God by keeping the law, never succeeded. Why not?
> Because they were trying to get right with God by
> keeping the law instead of by trusting in him. They
> stumbled over the great rock in their path. (Romans
> 9:30–32 NLTV)

Is there any wonder why the Pharisees and scribes were apoplectic with rage over this prodigal son story? Their God was not going to accept these heathen Gentiles. Those unclean infidels!

Another group of people was listening to Jesus's story. We can get so caught up in the highlights of this parable that we forget the lowlights. The tax collectors (the lowest of the low) and "the sinners" (pagans and atheists) were listening to the same story. Hearing how the father received his wayward son had to encourage their hearts. Surely hope began to rise in their souls. They had never heard about a God like this. Judgement and retribution were all they had ever heard about. They knew God loved the up-and-out, but they did not believe he loved the down-and-out:

> [For] the Son of Man has come to seek and to save
> that which is lost. (Luke 19:10 NKJV)

The prodigal sons (the Gentiles) were included in that which is lost.

Many people claim to believe in God, but they have no idea what kind of God they believe in. This story serves as a window into God's heart. If you want to know what God thinks about you, spend time in this parable. If you want to know how God sees you, make yourself at home in this story. If you want to know how God feels about you, pay close attention to how he goes after the lost sheep and the lost piece of silver and how he receives the prodigal son. Listen to how he responds to his eldest son's ranting about the favored treatment the prodigal son received when he came home. Maybe it would be a good idea if we spent less time on Facebook and more time in the Holy Book. If you do, you will find the answer to these questions. He is a loving and forgiving God.

There is one more character in this story that is overlooked by most. It is the fatted calf. This calf made a huge contribution to the homecoming celebration. Who do you think hated to see the return of the prodigal son more: the elder brother or the fatted calf?

> You search the Scriptures because you think they give you eternal life. But the Scriptures point to me! Yet you refuse to come to me to receive this life. (John 5:39–40 NLT)

Jesus speaks these words to the Jews who are harassing him for breaking Sabbath rules. They were even looking for ways to kill him because he broke the Sabbath and had the unmitigated gall to call God his Father, making himself equal with God (John 5:16–18 NLT).

The entire Bible, from Genesis to Revelation, is one big finger that points to Jesus. If this is true, and Jesus says it is, then the fatted calf deserves some attention. Jesus told this story long before barbed wire fences had been thought of, and cattle were allowed to roam free as they grazed. A few young calves were kept confined and fed so they would be plump and ready for a celebration. Fattened calves were usually associated with feasts and special celebrations:

> Again, he sent out other servants, saying, "Tell those who are invited, 'See, I have prepared my dinner;

my oxen and *fatted cattle* are killed, and all things
are ready. Come to the wedding.'" (Matthew 22:4
NKJV; emphasis added)

All of humanity is invited to this celebration, but not everyone
will accept the invitation.

Since all scripture points to Jesus, the fatted calf in Luke 16 must
be pointing to Jesus. He is the fattened calf of sacrifice. Jesus made
the greatest sacrifice for the celebration of sinners who have repented
and been placed where they belong:

For He made Him who knew no sin, to be sin for
us, that we might become the righteousness of God
in Him. (2 Corinthians 5:21 NKJV)

Jesus took our sin and shame upon himself so that we could
be a part of his forever family. As children of God, all birthright
privileges belong to us. We have a phenomenal inheritance.

The prodigal son may have squandered his livelihood, but he
did not lose his inheritance. He thought he had. The Pharisees and
scribes thought he should have too. This is why he said to himself,
"I'll ask my father to make me one of his hired servants" (Luke
15:19 NKJV). A servant is not entitled to an inheritance. When he
returned home, his father treated him like what he was: a son. The
father never mentioned his past. The important thing is the present.
The youngest son was back where he belonged, and his inheritance
was fully intact.

It is impossible for you to go back to the beginning of your life
and change your prodigal days, but you can start where you are at
this time and change your ending. No matter how far you have
walked away from God, the return trip is only one step. Turn your
heart toward home. The Father is ready and willing to receive you
with open arms. It's time to party.

CHAPTER  TEN

# NO GREATER LOVE

---

## Whatever God Is, He Is Completely

G od is good. Whatever God is, he is completely. Since God is good, he is completely good. The scriptures declare that it is the *goodness* of God that leads to repentance:

> Don't you see how wonderfully kind, tolerant, and patient God is with you? Does this mean nothing to you? Can't you see that *his kindness* is intended to turn you from your sin? (Romans 2:4 NLT; emphasis added)

If there is any one thing that we can glean from the parable of the prodigal son, it is the love God has for the world:

> For God loved the world so much that He gave his one and only Son, so that everyone who believes in him will not perish but have eternal life. (John 3:16 NLT)

You are included in this verse. God loves you so much that he gave his one and only Son to die on a cross so you can live—and he did this while you were in your sinning state and wanted nothing to do with him (Romans 5:8 NKJV). This kind of love is unfathomable by the human mind. It is beyond our ability to comprehend. The beautiful thing is that we don't have to understand; all we have to do is accept and receive it.

## God's Goodness Is Not Weakness

We must never perceive God's goodness and grace as weakness. Anyone and everyone who rejects Jesus Christ as their Lord and Savior will one day find out how strong goodness and grace really are. It takes incredible strength to love the unlovable. The love the father lavished on both sons in the parable Jesus told reveals his strength. He loved those who ran from him. He loved those who walked away from him. He loved those who felt rejected and unlovable, and he loved those who tried to kill him.

Everyone needs his love, and no one is beyond his love:

> The wicked are estranged from the womb. (Psalm 58:3 NKJV)

The word *estranged* means separation, alienated, or hostile. It did not take long for us to become sinners; we were born sinners. This is why Jesus said to Nicodemus, "You must be born from above" (John 3:3 NKJV). Everyone must have a second birth day. This is something Nicodemus did not understand. What did Jesus mean when he told him that he had to be born again? Nicodemus was thinking about a physical birth, but Jesus was talking about a spiritual birth.

> For the message of the cross is foolishness to *those who are perishing*, but to us who are being saved it

is the power of God. (1 Corinthians 1:18 NKJV; emphasis added)

Notice what Paul says about those who believe the message of the cross is foolishness. He did not say they think it is foolish; they actually believe it is foolish. These people are perishing now. Can a person be dead and living at the same time? Yes. A person can be alive physically and dead spiritually. Our physical lives come from our physical births. Our spiritual lives come from our spiritual births. This is why Jesus told Nicodemus that he had to be born again if he wanted to see the kingdom of God. We are not physical beings who have spirits. We are spiritual beings who live in bodies. Our physical lives are temporary, but our spiritual lives are eternal.

God the Father did not send his Son Jesus into this world to make bad people good. He came to make dead people alive:

And you He made alive, who were dead in trespasses and sins. (Ephesians 2:1 NKJV)

Paul says this again in verse 5. What does a dead person need? Do they need forgiveness or life? If you get the answer to this question right, everything else will begin to fall in to place. I'll give you a hint if you are still mulling it over. A dead person needs life. Jesus said, "I have come that they may have life, and that they may have it more abundantly" (John 10:10 NKJV). There is no greater love!

## The Significance of One

The significance of one is important to the Father. The man who discovered one of his sheep missing still had ninety-nine left in his flock. Is one really that important? It is to our heavenly Father. The man left the ninety-nine and searched until he found the missing sheep. He lovingly brought it back to the flock on his shoulders and placed it where it belonged: with the other sheep and with the Father. This is the only place where a sheep can survive and thrive. We now have the answer to the question: What does God think about me?

The significance of one is important to the woman. The woman who found one of her silver coins missing could have said, "I sure miss the coin that is missing, but at least I have nine left." No. That one missing coin was so important to this woman that she lit a lamp and swept inside her house until she found the piece that was lost. She placed the piece of silver back where it belonged. We now have the answer to the question: How does God see me?

The significance of one is important to the father. One of his sons was not where he was supposed to be. Instead of being in his father's house, he was living a wild life in a faraway country. This father could have been thankful that he still had a son at home. When the prodigal son finally had his come-to-the-father moment, he put his speech together and headed home. This young man got the shock of his life. He was received with open arms of grace. A big celebration was given to celebrate the occasion. The father was thrilled to have his son back where he belonged. We now have the answer to the question: How does God feel about me?

You are significant to the heavenly Father, and he made provisions for you long before there was a planet earth. God took care of every problem outside of time before there was ever a problem inside of time:

> The Lamb slain from the foundation of the world. (Revelation 13:8 NKJV)

This is how significant you are to God. You may be one of billions of people, but he came looking for you. He will accept and receive you with the same open arms of grace as the father received his prodigal son. There is no greater love.

Let me share with you one more time what I have said in a previous chapter. In my almost fifty-years of ministry, I have been asked the same question numerous times: If God is so good, then why does he send people to hell? The answer is simple. God does not send people to hell. He has never sent anyone to hell, and he will never send anyone to hell. A person goes to hell because they refuse to accept his invitation to life.

God has gone to great extremes to make you aware of his love for you. Because he has gifted you with a free will, where you spend eternity is your choice. You decide where you will spend eternity: with him or separated from him. It's your choice. I would encourage you to choose wisely. As long as you are still breathing, it is not too late for you.

## Some Things Are Past Finding Out

What about people who live in places where the Gospel of the good news was never preached? What about those who were never given the opportunity to receive Christ? These are questions I have been asked over the years. There are some things we need to leave in the hands of the Lord. If we know he is completely good, we can trust him. This may be a good idea since he is infinite, and we are finite:

> *He does great things past finding out,* Yes wonders without number. (Job 9:10 NKJV; emphasis added)

> "For my thoughts are not your thoughts, Nor are your ways My ways," says the Lord. "For as the heavens are higher than your ways, And My thoughts than your thoughts." (Isaiah 55:8–9 NKJV)

If we know that God is good, and whatever he is, he is completely, then we can leave the answers to these questions to him.

You cannot control God or the situations and circumstances in this world—past, present, or future. All you can do is decide what you are going to do with the good news of Jesus Christ. You can't make this decision for anyone else, and no one can make it for you. When it is all said and done, you will give an account for you—not for others. Where you spend eternity will be decided on this side of life. Another way to say it would be that the decision to accept or reject Jesus while you are in this physical realm will determine where you spend eternity in the spiritual realm. You will not be given a do-over. There is no way you can go back to the beginning and change anything, but you can start where you are now and change your ending. If you are still breathing, it is not too late for you. There is no greater love.

When the Bible says that God is love, it doesn't mean God is only love (1 John 4:8, NKJV). God's love is just one of his many attributes: God is light; God is a consuming fire; ad infinitum. There's one thing we do know about God: he is indescribable. Your mind will short-circuit if you try to thoroughly define him. When we try to explain something that is inexplicable, it can be very frustrating. How do you explain God? Any volunteers?

Our focus study for the day was in *pneumatology*, the branch of Christian theology concerned with the Holy Spirit. I will never forget what my seminary professor said to us about the Holy Trinity: "If you try to explain the Trinity, you will lose your mind. If you deny the Trinity, you will lose your soul." This is the answer I gave on our test. Since I was simply regurgitating what my professor had told us, I figured I had a shot at slipping it by him. Just in case you are wondering, my answer was not accepted. I think he wrote something like this: "Good try, but no cigar."

God's love is universal, and at the same time, his love is personal. God loves the world, but in particular, he loves you. Augustine said, "He loves each one of us as if there were only one of us." God loves those who are easy to love, and he loves those who are difficult to love. His love for us is greater than any sin in us. When we get a revelation of this, we will not be sinless, but we will sin less. There is no greater love.

I was leading a breakout session on new creation identity during a conference, and the room was filled with pastors and church staff workers. During the session, I made the comment that ministry would be awesome if you did not have to deal with people. In unison, there was one resounding "Amen!" I was trying to be funny, but everyone in the room was in agreement with what I said. Charlie Brown had the same attitude: "I love mankind; it's people I can't stand." I hope you know that I am being facetious. I would not be in the ministry today if I really believed this.

Karl Barth (1886–1968) was a German-born Swiss Reformed theologian. He visited one of our seminaries on one of his trips to the United States.

During a question and answer session, a seminary student stood and asked, "Dr. Barth, what is the most important truth you have learned as a theologian?"

Dr. Barth's answer was quick: "Jesus loves me, this I know, for the Bible tells me so." He could have mesmerized the class by revealing some specific idiosyncrasies of doctrines and theology he had discovered over the years. Instead, what moved him the most was the love God has for him. Even theologians are moved by the simplicity of God's love. There is no greater love.

## What a Friend We Have in Jesus

There were many horrific events that took place during the Vietnam war. I was in Vietnam in 1968, and I saw firsthand how cruel war can be for the innocent. There were many friendly fire mishaps that injured and killed innocent people, including children. Here is my account of one of those unfortunate accidents.

An eight-year-old orphan girl had been severely wounded by friendly fire. An American military doctor and nurse were called to help with medical treatment. After assessing the little girl's condition, they believed the little girl would die if she did not receive a blood transfusion—and get it fast. Tests showed that none of the American military personnel had the right blood type, but several of the uninjured orphans did.

The doctor was able to speak a little broken Vietnamese, but it was not enough to communicate effectively. The nurse could only speak a little French, which she had learned in high school. Between the doctor and the nurse and a lot of sign language, they tried to explain to the frightened children that unless they could replace the blood the young girl lost, she would certainly die. They asked the children if anyone would volunteer to give some of their blood.

Not fully understanding what the medical staff was asking, the children sat in silence.

After what seemed to be an eternity, a boy raised his hand reluctantly.

"Oh, thank you," the nurse said in French. "What is your name?"

"Heng," he said in a low monotone voice. Heng was laid on a pallet, his arm was swabbed with alcohol, and a needle was inserted into his arm. This little boy remained still and silent. After a short period of time, he began to sob quietly. He took his free hand and covered his face in an attempt not to be heard. His sobs turned into a steady cry. He tried to disguise his crying by placing his hand over his mouth.

The medical team became very concerned. Something was terribly wrong.

A Vietnamese nurse arrived to help the American medical team, and seeing that the little boy was stressed, she spoke to him in Vietnamese. The little boy said something, and the nurse answered him in a soothing voice.

It did not take long before the little boy stopped crying and stared at the Vietnamese nurse. When she gave him an affirming nod, a look of relief swept over the little boy's face. The nurse looked up at the medical team and said, "He thought he was dying. He misunderstood you. He thought you had asked him to give all his blood so the little girl could live."

The military nurse asked, "Why would he be willing to do that?"

The Vietnamese nurse repeated the question to the little boy, and he answered simply, "She is my friend."

This gives us a tiny glimpse of the incomprehensible love God has for us:

> Greater love has no one than this, than to lay down one's life for his friends. (John 15:13 NKJV)

Jesus gave his life so we could live. His death certificate made it possible for us to receive our birth certificates. What a friend we have in Jesus.

A friend is someone who knows all about you and still loves you. A friend will support you when you are right and has the courage to tell you when you are wrong. A true friend knows your faults but chooses to magnify your strengths:

> There are friends who destroy each other, but *a real friend sticks closer than a brother.* (Proverbs 18:24 NLTV; emphasis added)

Jesus is this friend who sticks closer than a brother. No one knows you better than he does, and he still loves you. He knows your every weakness, but he is quick to point out your strengths. He supports you when you are right, and he loves you so much that he is willing to tell you the truth when you are wrong—even if it is painful. There is no greater love. What a friend we have in Jesus.

## Love Covers

I cannot imagine the body odor the prodigal son must have had when his father grabbed him in his arms and loved on him. Jesus told us that the father kissed him repeatedly. His son had been living with pigs. You cannot live with pigs without getting some swine on you any more than you can clean out a chimney and not get soot on you. His clothes had to have been soiled and stained by his sinful lifestyle. The filth and uncleanness did not impede the father from loving on his wayward son. The prodigal son's past did not keep the father from receiving and welcoming him home.

The first thing the father did was cover him with the best robe. There were no instructions given for him to bathe and clean up first, so he would be worthy and presentable to receive the robe. The robe covered the sin of his past. The best robe that was placed on the son represented the unconditional love the father had for his son. The father loved him before there was any guarantee the son would love him back. The son could have come home to beg for more money.

This is exactly what Paul was saying to the believers who lived in Rome:

> For when we were still without strength, in due time Christ died for the ungodly. For scarcely for a righteous man will one die; yet perhaps for a good man someone would even dare to die. But God demonstrates His own love toward us, in that while we were still sinners, Christ died for us. (Romans 5:6–8 NKJV)

These verses are screaming with the love that God has for the lost and out-of-place soul. Christ died for us when we were still in our sinning state. He died for us when we did not want anything to do with him. Even though we were soiled and stained by our sinful lifestyles, even though we smelled like sin, God embraced us and loved on us. We were covered in robes of righteousness. Love covers a multitude of sins (1 Peter 4:8 NKJV).

## Love Removes

Here's the beauty of the new covenant that God has with his children. Our sins have not been *covered*—they have been *removed*:

> As far as the east is from the west, So far has He removed our transgressions from us. (Psalm 103:12 NKJV)

The Word of God does not say that our sins have been removed as far as the north is from the south. North to south is a measurable distance; east to west is not. If you travel north, you can go just so far until you are heading south, but it is not so with east and west. East and west will never meet. No matter how far you travel east, you will always be going east. God's love removes our sins that far.

> For I will be merciful to their unrighteousness, and their sins and *their lawless deeds I will remember no more.* (Hebrews 8:12 NKJV; emphasis added)

If God is omniscient, is it possible for him to not remember our sins. If it were possible for him to forget something, he would not be who he says he is. The word *remember* can mean to reattach. Once God forgives us our sins, he will never reattach them to us. The father never reminded the prodigal of his sins. Love removes.

It is time for us to recognize our new creation identity in Christ. We are no longer sinners who still need to be forgiven. We are saints who sometimes sin. *Sin consciousness* will lead you away from God. *Grace consciousness* draws you into a deeper awareness of who you are in Christ.

## Love Draws

The world is filled with lost souls, the people who are out of place, but the love of God draws home the lost sheep, the lost silver, and the lost sons and daughters. The heart of the Father is toward you. When sinners has their pigpen, come-to-the-Father moment, they find there is more grace in the Father's heart than there is sin in their lives.

Our heavenly Father is always ready to celebrate the return of a sinner who repents and comes home. He still has plenty of best robes, sandals, rings, and fatted calves. God's thoughts are always on you (Psalm 139:17–18 NKJV). He is looking for you to come home where you belong—with Him. There is plenty of room in the Father's house (John 14:1–6 NKJV).

Our heavenly Father has his heart set on you. For God loves you so much, that He gave His only Son, Jesus, that if you will believe in Him, trust Him with your life, you will never die. You will spend eternity with Him (John 3:16 NKJV). You may have wasted your livelihood on riotous living, but you have not lost your inheritance. It is possible to become self-righteous and legalistic—and still be loved by the Father

You should now have a better understanding about what God thinks about you, how God sees you, and how God feels about you. If you do, you cannot help but love him back.

# AFTERTHOUGHTS

Sin would not be so attractive if wages were paid immediately. As long as we are in this world, we will experience constant distractions. These distractions are designed to draw us away from reality. Reality is whatever God says. When we get away from God's Word, we are no longer living in reality—no matter how convincing it may appear. Whatever the Word of God calls sin, our opinion does not matter.

The bright lights of the faraway country will always be appealing to the flesh. Its promise of happiness, found in living life without boundaries, is a lie. Believing this lie is the first step in the wrong direction. Once the tentacles of this world's system grab ahold on you, it will draw you in slowly and gradually and squeeze the life out of you. Unless you come to your senses, it's only a matter of time before it robs you of all your dignity. It will not let you go until you spend it all. The world has plenty of pigpens available for those who want to test the limits.

## Free to Choose

God has gifted us with a free will. This incredible gift can be our greatest blessing or our biggest curse. I do not know of anyone who would appreciate being loved by someone who does not love them by choice. What kind of relationship would we have if we were devoid of the ability to choose to love someone? It would be mechanical and very unfulfilling. Everyone wants to be loved and appreciated by people whose desire is to love them. This is the cry of the human heart, knowingly or unknowingly.

This is precisely why the father did not try to talk his youngest son out of leaving home for the faraway country. The father knew his son was making the wrong decision by setting out on his own. He knew how cruel the world can be. He knew his son was not mature enough or ready to be on his own, yet he still let him go:

> And He [God] gave them their request, But sent leanness into their soul. (Psalm 106:15 NKJV; emphasis added)

Sometimes the worst thing that can happen to us is for God to give us what we ask for. If you find this hard to believe, you might want to have a conversation with the prodigal son.

The father's oldest son had free will too. He could have chosen to participate in the celebration that was being held for his brother's return or not. Even though the father explained to the elder brother why they were having a homecoming celebration for his brother, he did not demand or force his oldest son to join the party. That would have violated the elder brother's free will. The father allowed him to make his own choice.

The same is true with us. One of the many things that separates us from all animal forms is our free will. Because we have a free will, we are responsible for the choices we make in life—and we will give an account someday of the choices we have made. The most important choice we will ever make is to accept Jesus Christ as our Lord and Savior. Even though making the wrong choice has consequences for time and eternity, the Holy Spirit will not go against your will.

There is one thing we may not have considered. Until we say yes to the Lord's invitation to life, we have made a choice. That choice is to reject him. There is no middle ground with Jesus. The Word of God says that we are either scattering or gathering (Matthew

12:30 NKJV). We are for him or against him. We are in light or in darkness. We are saved or lost.

Some people say, "Well, I haven't made up my mind yet if I'm going to accept Jesus Christ as my Lord and Savior." When they say this, they have already made their choice. They have said no. Since we have a free will to choose, we can change our choice. As long as we are on this side of eternity, and breathing, we can change our no to a yes. Once we close our eyes in death, we will never escape the consequences of our choices.

Let's set aside theology for a moment and think our way through why accepting and receiving Jesus as Lord and Savior makes sense. If I believe there is a God who sent his Son, Jesus Christ, to this earth to demonstrate his love for me by dying on the cross and then raising him up on the third day, what do I lose if I believe that and it ends up not being true? If I trust what the Word of God says about repenting of my sins and confessing Jesus Christ as my Lord and Savior, then I find out it is not true when I die, what have I lost? Absolutely nothing.

What about a person who does not believe there is a God and that the Gospel is not true? When they die and discover it is true, what do they lose? I think the answer is obvious. They lose everything. We living today with the choices we made yesterday, and we will live tomorrow with the choices we make today. Where we spend eternity will be determined by the choice we make to accept or reject Jesus Christ. You have been gifted with a free will. Choose wisely. Where you spend eternity depends on it.

## The Father's Unconditional Love

God's love is unconditional. This is what the Pharisees and scribes could not handle. How can God love tax collectors, sinners, and someone like the prodigal son? They have proven they do not deserve to be loved. The God they believe in would not.

A young man stood in a seminary class and announced to the professor and his fellow students that he no longer believed in God.

The professor was unmoved by this young man's declaration. With kindness in his voice, he said, "Tell me about your God that you no longer believe in."

The young man said, "I can't believe in a God who would send people to hell, a God who is unloving and vengeful."

The professor replied, "I wouldn't believe in your God either. My God is loving and kind. My God is very gracious and long-suffering. My God is a God of love."

So many Christians are like the Pharisees and scribes. They have a pharisaical view of God. Their response to Jesus meeting with sinners reveals their hypocritical, censorious self-righteousness. Someone who has an elder brother spirit believes that God only has time for those who work hard at being righteous. To suggest that God will meet with reprobates is beyond their comfort zone. Their God would not receive and embrace someone as low as the prodigal son, much less celebrate their return. Justice? Yes. Grace? Absolutely not! They are more into stoning than restoring.

More and more prodigals would be coming home if they knew that God is a loving God. There is no faraway country beyond the limits of his love. Can anything ever separate us from Christ's love? Does it mean he no longer loves us if we have trouble or calamity or are persecuted, hungry, destitute, in danger, or threatened with death?

> As the Scriptures say, "For your sake we are killed every day; we are being slaughtered like sheep." (Romans 8:36 NLT)

No, despite all these things, overwhelming victory is ours through Christ. He loves us, and I am convinced that nothing can separate us from God's love:

> Neither death nor life, neither angels nor demons, neither our fears for today nor our worries about

tomorrow—not even the powers of hell can separate us from God's love. No power in the sky above or in the earth below—indeed, nothing in all creation will ever be able to separate us from the love of God that is revealed in Christ Jesus our Lord. (Romans 8:35–39 NLT)

Do you notice something conspicuous by its absence in these verses? Paul mentions the fears we may have today and the worries we may have tomorrow, but he does not mention the past. This is why the father did not say a word to his prodigal son about what he had done or where he had been. This is not important to the Father. He is more concerned with where you are and what you are doing. Your past may be brought up, but it will be brought up by the enemy of your soul, elder brothers, or the Pharisees and scribes. It will not be by the Lord. God is not mad at you. He is madly in love with you. How can you not love him back?

This is why the consequences are so severe for those who refuse to accept God's invitation to life. A person who rejects Christ will be separated from him forever. This separation does not happen because God is vindictive or revengeful. It is by one's own free will; a person chooses to be separated from God by rejecting his love. This has already been said, but it needs to be said again: once a person dies, they will never be given a second chance to get things right. Where you spend eternity will be decided before you die. Because you have a free will, you cannot blame anyone else for what happens to you when you take your last breath on this side of eternity.

## Ignorance Is Not Always Bliss

It amazes me that the elder son could share his father's home and *not* share his father's heart. This is more common than many people realize. It happens in families all the time—even in the family of faith. On the news, after some horrific family violence, a family member might say, "I guess we never really knew them."

Even though the elder brother was always with his father, he never really knew him. After a long, hard day in the fields, when the elder brother approached the house, he could hear the music and the dancing. When he found out why there was a celebration, it angered him. When he refused to go inside, his father went outside to where he was.

The elder brother began to make his case as to why he thought this celebration for the prodigal was not appropriate. In his speech, he made mention that he had never been given an opportunity to have a party to celebrate anything. He would not acknowledge the prodigal as being his brother. "This son of yours" was his choice of words (Luke 15:30 NKJV). If he had really known his father, he would not have been surprised or upset about how his father was honoring his youngest son's return home.

This truth is widespread in the family of faith today. It is possible for us to be with the Lord for years and not really know him. We don't know what he thinks about us. We don't know how he sees us or feels about us. It is possible for us to share his home but not share his heart. Most Christians believe the Father is hard to please and is cranky most of the time. To suggest he likes to party sounds offensive to their ears. According to Jesus, every time a sinner comes to the Father, there is one huge celebration in heaven:

> And he said to him, "Son, you are always with me,
> and all that I have is yours." (Luke 15:31 NKJV)

The first thing the father did was remind the elder brother that he was his son. If the elder brother was always with his father, then why didn't he know his father better? I think it is pretty obvious. He was so self-absorbed that he didn't have time to get to know his father. Just like the prodigal son, life was all about him. The center of his universe was himself. He knew his father's business and his home inside and out, but he did not know his father's heart.

The father reminds his eldest son about the intimacy they shared: "You have always been with me" (Luke 15:31 NKJV). I do tip my hat to the elder brother for his hard work and for his willingness to stay home. It's sad that he was working hard to get what he already had and to be who he already was. This sounds so familiar, doesn't it? So many Christians are working hard to become what Christ has already made them to be. They are working hard to get what they already have: birthright privileges. In the process, they burn out. They either run away or quit. They may keep doing what they have always done, but their hearts are no longer in it.

After reminding his eldest son about the intimacy they have as father and son, the father reminds him of his inheritance: "All that I have is yours" (Luke 15:31 NKJV). The elder brother has forgotten that when his brother demanded his share of their father's livelihood, he got his share too:

> And the younger of them said to his father, "Father, give me the portion of goods that falls to me." So he *divided to them* his livelihood. (Luke 15:12 NKJV; emphasis added)

The prodigal son got one-third, but the elder brother got two-thirds. Isn't it amazing how easy it is for us to forget what we do have because we are so focused on what we don't have—or think we need?

Here is another little tidbit worth noting. The prodigal son wasted his livelihood, but he did not lose his inheritance. This is how good our heavenly Father is. Even when we choose the prodigal lifestyle, for a season, when we repent and return, we find our inheritance is still intact. This is another reason why the elder brothers are so critical of prodigals coming home. They do not like how the father receives them. His arms of grace are always open to welcome the wayward who have chosen to come home.

## The End of the Story

Did the two sons ever reconcile? Did the boys get their acts together? Did they fall in love with their father? How did things turn out? We don't know because Jesus did not tell us. This is not how we like our stories to end. We don't like to be left hanging in suspense.

Could it be that Jesus did this on purpose? I am convinced he did. When it is all said and done, this parable is about us: you and me. How are we going to finish this story? What will be the ending that we write with our lives? We have been given the gift of free will. It becomes our choice. There is no way we can go back to the beginning of our stories and alter or change anything. It is what it is. However, we can start where we are in our stories and finish well. Life is not about where we have been or what we have done. It is what we are doing and where we are that matters. Put on your grace sandals—and finish your race well (Hebrews 12:1 NKJV).

We do know how most of the Pharisees and scribes ended their story:

> Now the Pharisees, who were lovers of money, also heard all these things, and they *derided* Him. (Luke 16:14 NKJV; emphasis added)

They laughed at Jesus. They hurled insults at him. They showed him no respect. They had their legal lines drawn to separate the Law from grace, and they were not about to cross to the grace side. They despised and ridiculed anyone who did.

Years ago, I had a friend who lived the prodigal life, and he lived it for most of his life. His life story had so much in common with the man's I shared in chapter 3. The majority of his life had been spent in riotous living in the backstreets of a large city in Texas. He was considered the lowest of the lows. Then it happened. A street evangelist, himself a recovered drug addict, shared the love and grace of the Father with my friend. Right there, in one of those dark alleys of this big city, he accepted and received Jesus as his Lord and Savior. His life was forever changed.

For a couple of years after his encounter with Christ, he lived in a home for recovering addicts. During this time, he felt the call of God on his life to preach the Gospel—and preach he did. It is reported that he won hundreds of street addicts to Christ. He was fearless in sharing the good news with those who lived in his former neighborhood: the dark back alleyways of this city. His personal testimony of finding God's grace touched the lives of many who were battling addictions. Many of his converts became preachers of the same Gospel of grace.

By the time I met him, he had been pastoring for a couple of years in a small church outside the city limits of the town I was pastoring in. He faithfully served the people of that church for several years. If you did not know his story, you would not have a clue about his prodigal past. I sat there in rapt attention the day he shared his life experience with me. My friend was so full of God that he could not help but weep when he talked about God's grace and goodness. This man was so gentle and kind. He was a phenomenal pastor and an incredible husband to a wonderful lady.

One day, he met me in the parking lot of the church I was pastoring and shared some disturbing news. He was dying. His past life had taken its toll on his body. We stood there for a long time, talking, praying, and crying. We talked about heaven and how incredible it was going to be to see our Jesus face-to-face. My friend was not afraid of his impending fate. He was actually looking forward to his homegoing. It was not long after our parking lot talk that he transitioned from this earthly realm to heaven. He is more alive today than he ever was while living in this world.

There was no way my friend could go back to the beginning of his life and change anything. If he could have, he surely would have. What he could do, and did, was start where he was and finish well.

And finish well he did. His life was not about where he had been or what he had done. His life was about where he was and what he was doing. His story ended well—by choice.

I am convinced this is why Jesus did not tie up all the loose ends of the parable he told in Luke. He leaves it up to us to finish. How will we end it? Since we have been gifted with a free will, we can choose how our life stories end. We are writing our own epitaphs with our lives. We can all end well if we choose:

> For I am already being poured out as a drink offering, and the time of my departure is at hand. I have fought the good fight, I have finished the race, I have kept the faith. Finally, there is laid up for me the crown of righteousness, which the Lord, the righteous Judge, will give to me on that Day, and not to me only but also to all who have loved His appearing (2 Timothy 4:6–8 NKJV)

Paul finished his race a lot different than he started. He became the very thing he tried so hard to eradicate: a Christian. Paul could not change how he started, but he could change how he ended.

They came in late for the service and took the very back seats. This made it easy for them to leave when the service ended without being detected. And they did.

When they were about to drive away, the man said to his wife, "I feel I need to go back inside and talk to that guy."

She responded, "If you think the Lord wants you to, go talk to him."

I was standing close to the front entrance of the building when I saw this guy walking toward me with his hand extended. I had no clue that this handshake would bond us together as a father and spiritual son. During our brief introduction, he gave me the CliffsNotes version of his life. We made an appointment to meet the next day. He showed up thirty minutes early, and we spent more than three hours in deep conversation. He poured out his life story to me: the good, the bad, and the very ugly.

This young man had spent his entire life chasing after his dream. He was so focused on making it to where he wanted to go that nothing else in life mattered. All of his hard work and determination were about to pay off. He was on the threshold of realizing his dream when everything went south. By no fault of his own, something unforeseen happened that ended his pursuit. His dream went down the tubes, and his identity did as well. When he lost his dream, he lost himself.

With his dreams gone, his pursuit for identity went in another direction. He tried to find his identity in drugs, partying, bright lights of the faraway country, and unhealthy relationships. The hole he was digging for himself only got deeper. His despair was so great that he became the slave of meth (methamphetamine).

Loving family members stepped in and had him committed to an interdiction program. This was the young man who shook my hand on that Sunday morning and spent more than three hours in my office the next day. I ended up giving him office space next to mine. We usually kept the doors to both offices open, and for the next three years, I poured my life into him. I dragged this poor young man with me all over the world. He and I have seen some incredible moves of the Spirit of God. We witnessed God doing things in Uganda that most of us only read about—and then wonder if the one reporting it is telling the truth. My spiritual son has shared his testimony to thousands of people. He wrote the foreword to my book, *The Scam*, which has given his testimony more exposure.

If you were to ask my spiritual son if there was anything he would change in his life, I'm sure he would say yes. However, you cannot change the past. That is why it is called the past. The good news is that you can start where you are and change how your story ends. This is what my spiritual son is doing. I am so proud of him. He is a great husband to a beautiful lady, an incredible dad to four sweet girls, and a successful entrepreneur. He is a man who loves the Lord. You will not find many people who can match his sweet spirit and generous heart.

In Christ, he found the identity he was pursuing with so much passion. He will be the first to tell you that real life is found in Christ and Christ alone. My spiritual son may have had a rough and rocky start—he certainly made some poor choices—but he is writing the ending to the parable Jesus told about the prodigal son with grace and dignity. He may have lost some livelihood, but he did not lose his inheritance:

> For to me, to live is Christ and to die is gain.
> (Philippians 1:21 NKJV)

How is it possible for anyone to say with such bold confidence that for me to live is Christ and to die is gain? It's only possible by knowing what God thinks about you, how God sees you, and how God feels about you. Hopefully, by now, you know. It may be time for you to come home.

# ABOUT THE AUTHOR

Wayne Kniffen has been a pastor for almost fifty years. For the past twenty-one years, he has been the lead pastor of a church in the Texas Panhandle. He has become a prolific writer in his senior years. The following are his own words: "The Lord told me that I am in my last season, but it will be the most productive season of my life. Let what you leave live on." Kniffen has tried to be faithful to this revelation. He has written nine books in the span of fourteen months. *The Scam, The Exchange: God's Quid Pro Quo,* and *If We Only Knew* have already been published and are available at most book retailers.

Kniffen has traveled all over the world sharing the message of new creation identity. He is convinced that most believers live their entire lives without discovering who they are in Christ. He is quick to point out that not knowing your new creation identity will not make you less than a child of God, and knowing it will not make you more than a child of God, but knowing who Christ has made you to be will free you to enjoy all of your birthright privileges.

For personal contact: waynekniffen@outlook.com.

Printed in the United States
by Baker & Taylor Publisher Services